Artur Juszczak
Robert Pęczkowski

Colour illustrations by
Artur Juszczak

Bell P-39 Airacobra

STRATUS

Published in Poland in 2011
by STRATUS s.c.
Po. Box 123,
27-600 Sandomierz 1, Poland
e-mail: office@mmpbooks.biz
for
Mushroom Model Publications,
3 Gloucester Close, Petersfield,
Hampshire GU32 3AX, UK.
E-mail: rogerw@mmpbooks.biz
© 2011 Mushroom Model
Publications.
http://www.mmpbooks.biz

All rights reserved. Apart from any fair dealing for the purpose of private study, research, criticism or review, as permitted under the Copyright, Design and Patents Act, 1988, no part of this publication may be reproduced, stored in a retrieval system, or transmitted in any form or by any means, electronic, electrical, chemical, mechanical, optical, photocopying, recording or otherwise, without prior written permission. All enquiries should be addressed to the publisher.

ISBN
978-83-61421-28-3

Editor in chief
Roger Wallsgrove

Editorial Team
Bartłomiej Belcarz
Artur Juszczak
James Kightly
Robert Pęczkowski

DTP
Robert Pęczkowski
Artur Juszczak

Colour Drawings
Artur Juszczak

Scale Plans
Marek Ryś

Printed by:
Drukarnia Diecezjalna,
ul. Żeromskiego 4,
27-600 Sandomierz
phone: +48 15 644 04 00
www.wds.pl marketing@wds.pl

PRINTED IN POLAND

Bibliography

Brown, E, Cpt.; *Wings of the Weird & Wonderful*, Airlife
Byk, G.; *Bell P-39 Airacobra in RAAF Service*, A Red Roo Models Publication, 1997.
Green, W.; *Fighters*, Vol. 4, Macdonald;
Gunston, B.; *Wings*, Orbis Publishing, "Bell Aircraft: The Innovators";
Johnsen, F. A.; *Bell P-39/P-63 Airacobra & Kingcobra*, WarbirdTech Series Vol. 17, Speciality Press, North Branch, 1998;
Kinzley, B.; *P-39 Airacobra*, In Detail & Scale vol. 63, Squadron/Signal Publications, Carrollton, 1999;
McDowell, E.; *P-39 Airacobra in Action*, Aircraft No 43, Squadron/Signal Publications, Carrollton, 1980;
Roman, V.; *Aerocobry Vstupayut v Boi*, Aerohobbi, Kiev, 1993;
Tomalik, J.; *Bell P-39 Airacobra cz.1*, Monografie Lotnicze Nr 58, AJ-Press, Gdańsk, 1999;
Tomalik, J.; *Bell P-63 Kingcobra XFL-1 Airabonita, P-39 Airacobra cz. 2*, Monografie lotnicze Nr 59, AJ-Press, Gdańsk, 2001;

Get in the picture!
Do you have photographs of historical aircraft, airfields in action, or original and unusual stories to tell? MMP would like to hear from you! We welcome previously unpublished material that will help to make MMP books the best of their kind. We will return original photos to you and provide full credit for your images. Contact us before sending us any valuable material: *rogerw@mmpbooks.biz*

Acknowledgements:
Author wish to acknowledge the kind assistance of the following:
The late Arthur Lochte, Mikael Orlog, Tomasz J. Kopański, Robert Zaborski, Przemysław Skulski, Wojciech Łuczak, Darryl Ford, Paweł Bondaryk,

Cover photo: P-39Q-5 Airacobra, G-CEJU, painted as serial 42-19993 Brooklyn Bum - 2nd personal aircraft of Lt. Peter A. McDermott, 82nd TRS, 71st TRG, Tadji aerodrome, New Guinea. Aircraft belonging to The Fighter Collection. (Paweł Bondaryk)

Title page photo: P-39D during maintenance in Australia, March 1944. (US National Archive)

Table of contents

Bibliography. 2
Introduction 5
P-39 Versions 8
Bell YP-39 Airacobra 8
Bell P-39C Airacobra 10
Bell P-39D Airacobra 14
Airacobra I for the RAF, P-400 15
Bell P-39D-1 & D-2 Airacobra 20
Bell XP-39E Airacobra 24
Bell P-39F Airacobra 25
Bell P-39J Airacobra 30
Bell P-39G/H Airacobra 30
Bell P-39K Airacobra 30
Bell P-39L Airacobra 33
Bell P-39M Airacobra 35
Bell P-39N Airacobra 37
Bell P-39Q Airacobra 40
Soviet "improvements" and operating instructions. 48
Official USAAF P-39 Performance Figures 50
Detailed P-39D specification according to Russian tests 51
Aircraft tests in USSR 52
Technical description 53
List of Soviet P-39 Aces 64
Detail photos 65
Fuselage 65
Canopy 81
Cockpit 84
Wing 100
Engine 108
Tail 115
Undercarriage 119
Armament 129
Colour Profiles 135

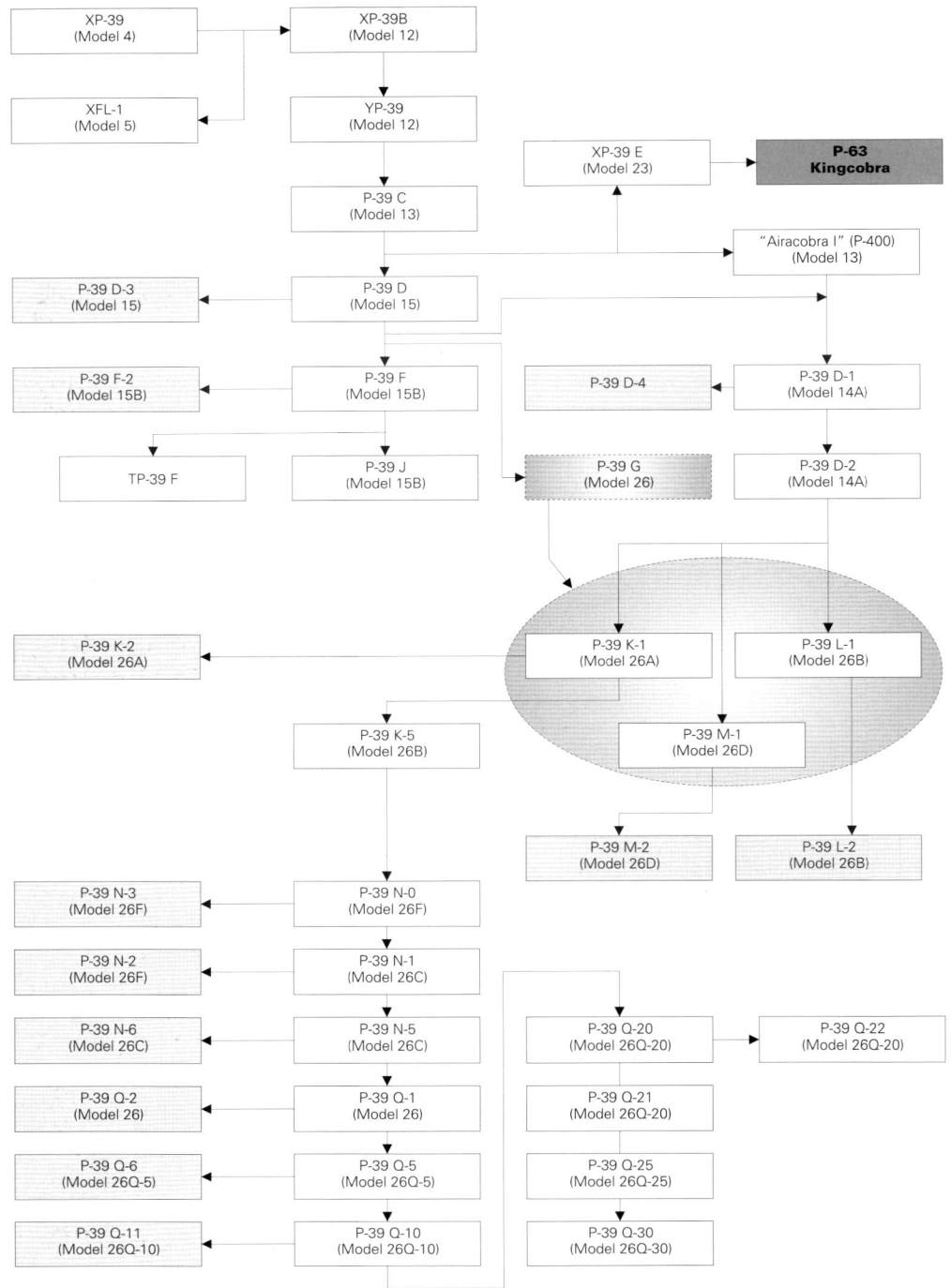

Introduction

The XP-39 Airacobra prototype was rolled out at Wright Field on 6 April 1939. Essentially the aeroplane was designed around the new 37-mm Oldsmobile cannon, and this was the second project from Bell to use this weapon (first was the Airacuda). Initially it was assumed that the cannon would be located aft of the engine (this being positioned conventionally, at the front) with the cockpit as far aft as possible. Though Bell Aircraft had only been founded four years earlier, they were innovators in the American fighter market, as exemplified by the XFM-1 Airacuda, P-39 Airacobra and -63 Kingcobra, XFL-1 Airabonita, P-59 Airacomet and XP-77: all types with at least one, and often more, unique features.

Bell's chief designer, Robert Woods, opted for the concept to locate the engine in the centre, so that the nose of the aeroplane was available for the very powerful (by the standards of the time) armament. It should be noted, however, that such a position for the engine was not an original idea. This concept had been tested by Koolhoven in the Netherlands, and Westlands in England, albeit without much success, due to an insufficiently powerful engines and inadequate technology. However the idea of the centrally mounted engine also allowed for a tricycle undercarriage, something gaining popularity in the USA. In the case of the Airacobra, this position required a 3m long shaft and gearing to pass under the pilot from the engine to the propeller.

In his design, Wood used the new 1,150 hp Allison V-1710 engine with the new B-5 turbocharger. Fitting this supercharger would allow the aeroplane to achieve high performance at high altitudes. Maximum power output would be achieved at 20,000 feet, as it was in the XP-38. These plans were realised when on 6 April the XP-39 reach a speed of 390 mph. During subsequent tests it even approached 400 mph (398). The fighter also displayed an excellent rate of climb: 20,000 feet in 5 minutes! Thus this unusual-looking little plane caused quite a stir in aviation circles. No aeroplane in Europe was able to match this performance. None other was ready for production, either. It has to be stressed, though, that the XP-39 was unarmed, it had no armour, and no self-sealing tanks (in fact these latter two items were not required by the USAAC).

Unfortunately, although excellent in performance, the aeroplane was not without flaws. The small fin led to problems with longitudinal stability. In common with many aircraft designed at this period, Woods had

XP-39, prototype, serial 38-326 at Wright Field just after delivery. (US National Archive)

YP-39 during tests at Langley, NASA. (NASA)

also selected an aerofoil section which turned out to be not best suited to the higher end of the aircraft's speed envelope. These problems could be cured, though, and in fact the fin was later reshaped and enlarged. However, the aerofoil was not changed until the advent of the P-63 Kingcobra, that aeroplane having a laminar flow wing.

After factory tests the XP-39 was handed over to engineers at Wright Field, and they modified the aeroplane. At the time when the aeroplane was undergoing tests, the AAF favoured "streamlined forms" as the way of improving an aeroplane's performance, quite logically, considering the relatively low power outputs of the engines of the 1930s. Wright Field considered that reducing the frontal drag would lead to a substantial improvement in performance. However, they went too far in the case of the XP-39. The NACA engineers decided that the Bell turbo-supercharger air intakes caused too much drag, and had to be removed. Additionally, the cockpit was lowered, the wing was clipped by 2 ft, and the fuselage stretched by 1 ft. A less powerful Allison engine with a single-stage mechanical supercharger replaced the turbocharged engine. This deprived the aeroplane of its original advantage, the excellent high altitude performance, though the low-level manoeuvrability was enhanced. Moreover, these changes shifted the centre of gravity forward, further reducing the already low stability of the aeroplane. Thus, the Wright Field experts, in their attempts to improve the aeroplane, actually removed or degraded several of its original advantages.

Larry Bell and Robert Wood were not happy with these "improvements", but could not afford a fight to retain the aeroplane in its original form. Bell Aircraft was on the edge of bankruptcy. With only 15 aircraft to sell, Bell was in debt. Neither Bell nor Woods wanted to lose an order for the new aeroplane. In order to maintain the financial stability of the company, they accepted all the suggested changes. As America needed modern aeroplanes quickly, with war looking imminent, this was convenient for everybody.

Bell obtained P-39 orders from France, receiving US$2 million in advance and $11 million more on delivery. Later that same year (1940) Bell received an order for 1,000 P-39C and P-39D aircraft from the USAAF, plus orders from the RAF based on the exceptional performance figures quoted by Bell for the XP-39. These production versions were progressively fitted with armour and self-sealing tanks, which degraded the performance even further. Without the turbocharger, just with the mechanical supercharger, the Airacobra was a mediocre fighter by current standards, especially above 10,000 ft. It has to be stressed that the early versions of the Allison V-1170 engine without turbo-supercharger were significantly less powerful than the engine of the prototype XP-39, and the RAF received an aircraft weighing over a ton more than the machine that gave the statistics Bell had provided.

The aeroplane was allegedly so difficult to control that it was said to enter flat spin if the pilot yawed the machine. Many other stores about its aerobatic handling were swapped in pilot's tents in the early dark days of WWII. However, with hindsight it is possible to say that the concentration of weight about the aircraft's c-of-g gave excellent manoeuvrability, but changes to this weight (for instance, firing off all the heavy cannon ammunition) would affect that handling. Furthermore, the 37 mm Colt M4 cannon would often jam after a few rounds were fired. Even worse, the British pointed out that gun fumes (including lethal carbon monoxide) collected in the cockpit, and that a burst from all weapons would throw off the magnetic compass reading. Not surprisingly, some British pilots refused to fly the aeroplane, and one of them even said that the aeroplane was more dangerous to the RAF than the *Luftwaffe*. These opinions would follow the aeroplane throughout its service - except in Russia!

The RAF admitted that the Airacobra was equal in performance to the Bf 109E low down, but by 1941 they needed an aeroplane able to cope with the latest *Luftwaffe* fighters at much higher altitudes. On the other hand, it has been stated that the problems 601 Sqn had with the type were more to do with its unconventional layout, a lack of appropriate induction to the unit, and teething problems which were not addressed properly because it was a foreign design.

Since the Russians were quite satisfied with the aeroplane's performance, or perhaps their need of fighter aircraft was greater than the shortcomings of the Airacobra, a large proportion of the P-39s produced was despatched there. It is worth noting, too, that most air combat on the Eastern Front took place at altitudes below 20,000 ft. One should also admit the skills of the Soviet pilots, who used these aircraft very effectively against the *Luftwaffe*. As will be seen later, the Soviets also modified their P-39s to improve their combat effectiveness.

The P-39 was also used in North Africa and Italy by units of the USAAF and other countries, including the Free French and Italians, up to the end of the war. The Airacobra was also used in the Pacific, as described in many press articles and books. However, in the latter theatre the "Iron Dog" was replaced with other aircraft as quickly as possible.

Born into a rapidly changing air warfare environment, the P-39 never really caught up with the changes required, resulting from the urgent lessons the USAAF and the RAF were being forced to learn. Coupled with some unusual stability effects caused by the engine being over the c-of-g, this caused the type to gain a reputation as a 'dangerous' machine. However, no less a test pilot that Capt. Eric 'Winkle' Brown stated: "I did manage to persuade our engineers to let me have a farewell flight in 28th March [1946], when I had a super fifty minute session of aerobatics over Farnborough to show the old lady still had a kick in her." And this was in a machine a Bell test pilot had condemned as 'clapped out.'! Coupled with a lack of recognition of the importance of designed-in armour, self-sealing fuel tanks and properly installed armament, the Bell fighters were never to gain popularity in the west. In conclusion, the P-39 was a relative failure because of errors by both the engineers and the establishment of the USAAF. Had the USAAC (Air Corps) not ordered removal of the turbo-supercharger from the XP-39, the USA could have entered the war with a potent fighter aeroplane. The later P-63 showed just how good the concept could be, yet by the time it appeared it was tarred with the same brush as the P-39 and saw no USAAF service – to the benefit of the V-VS, who took almost all the production!

P-39 Versions

The USAAC was satisfied that the low-altitude performance of the P-39 was sufficient, and that high altitude use was not going to be a requirement, and therefore directed that the twelve YP-39s be completed without turbochargers. These machines also featured radiator intakes in the wing roots rather than the fuselage sides, and the air intake on the dorsal spine.

The first YP-39 (serial no 40-027) was flown on 13 September, 1940 with the 1,090 hp V-1710-37 (E5) engine driving a Curtiss Electric propeller. The first few YP-39s were initially flown without armament, but the next machines were fitted with a 37 mm cannon with 15 rounds, two 0.50 in machine guns with 200 rounds per gun, and two 0.30 in machine guns with 500 rounds per gun. Armour protection was provided for the pilot. Empty and normal loaded weights rose to 5,042 pounds and 7,000 pounds, respectively. The perform-

Above: YP-39 with redesigned cooler. (via A. Lochte)
Below: YP-39, serial 40-27 at Buffalo airfield, October 1940. (US National Archive)

ance of the YP-39 dropped to a maximum speed of 368 mph at 15,000 feet. An altitude of 20,000 feet could be attained in 7.3 minutes. Service ceiling was 33,300 feet.

The thirteen YP-39s (serials 40-027~40-039) were delivered between 6 September and 16 December 1940. They were used only for evaluation and tests.

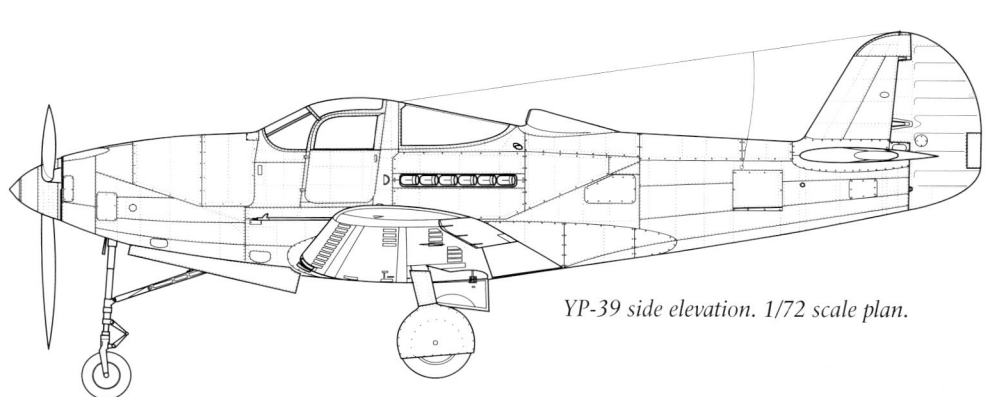

YP-39 side elevation. 1/72 scale plan.

YP-39 during tests at Langley. (NASA)

Bell P-39C Airacobra

The USAAC was gen-erally pleased with the Airacobra, and an initial order for 80 production aircraft (Bell Model 13) was issued on 10 August 1939 under Contract AC13383.

The USAAC firstly allocated the new designation of P-45 to these machines, even though they were almost identical to the YP-39 test aircraft. However, in the political climate of 1940, it was impossible for the USAAC to order any new aircraft, but it could order more examples of an already-existing model and the designation of the production Airacobra was changed to P-39C before the delivery of the first aircraft.

The first P-39C (Serial No 40-2971) flew in January 1941. The P-39C was identical to the YP-39, with the exception of the engine, which was a 1,150 hp Allison V-1710-35 (E4).

The Army discovered almost immediately that the P-39C was not combat ready, since it has no armour and self-sealing tanks. Because of that, only twenty P-39Cs were built - serial numbers 40-2971 to 40-2990. On September 14, 1940 the initial order for 80 P-39Cs was amended

Right: P-39C nose details.

Below: P-39C at Buffalo. (via A Lochte)

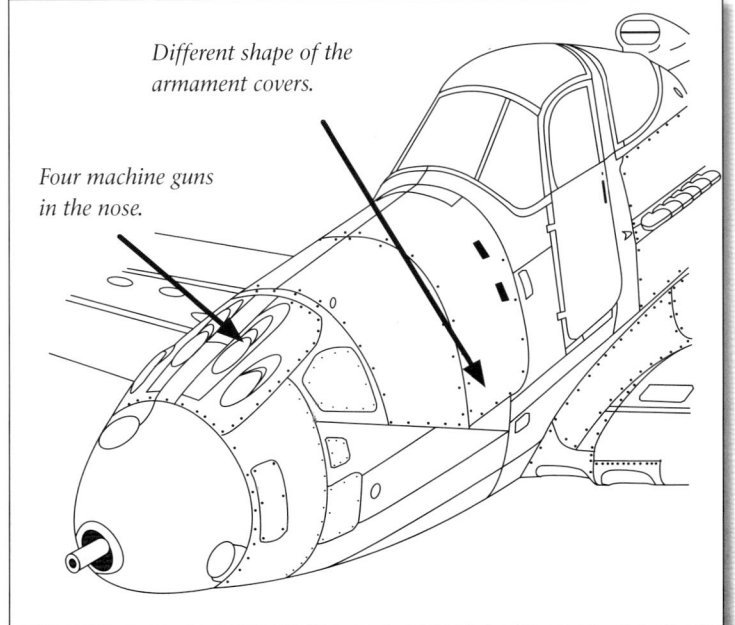

Different shape of the armament covers.

Four machine guns in the nose.

to provide for self-sealing fuel tanks. The remaining 60 planes of the order (serial numbers 40-2991 to 40-3050) were completed to this standard and were redesignated as P-39Ds.

Armament was one 37 mm cannon, two 0.50 in and two 0.30 in machine guns, all in the nose.
Serials were 40-2971~40-3050.

P-39C after delivery to a unit. (Stratus coll.)

P-39C side view. 1/72 scale.

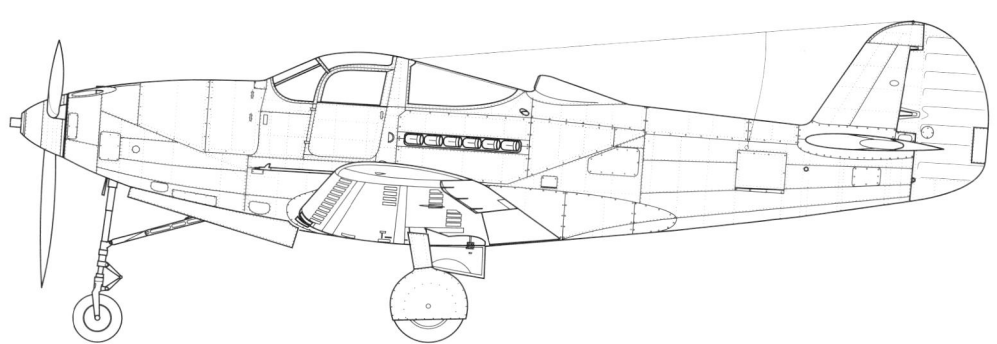

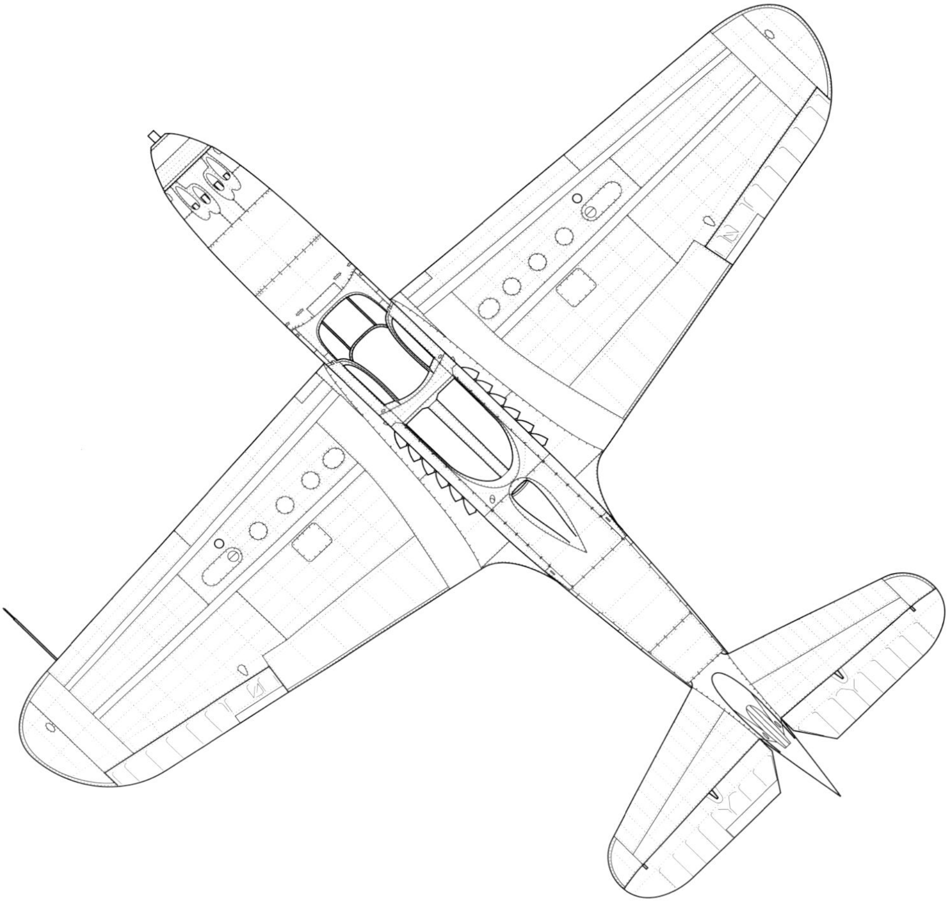

P-39C 1/72 scale plans.

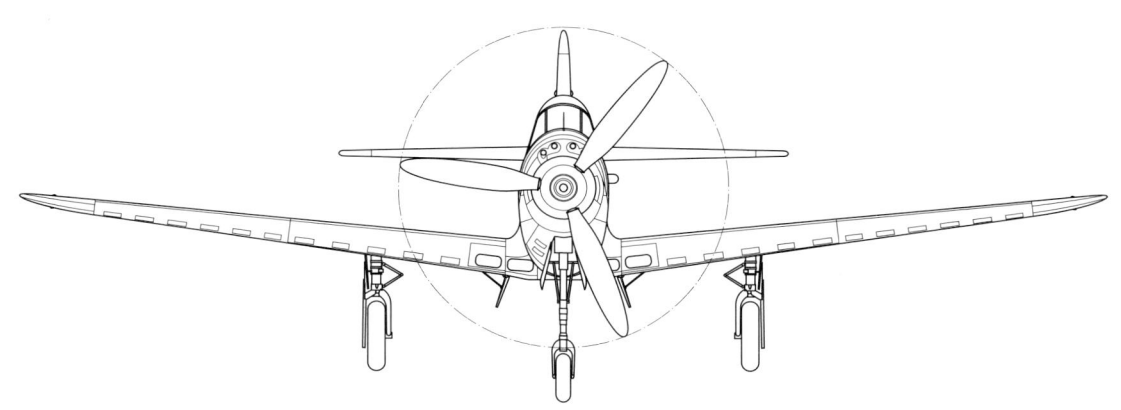

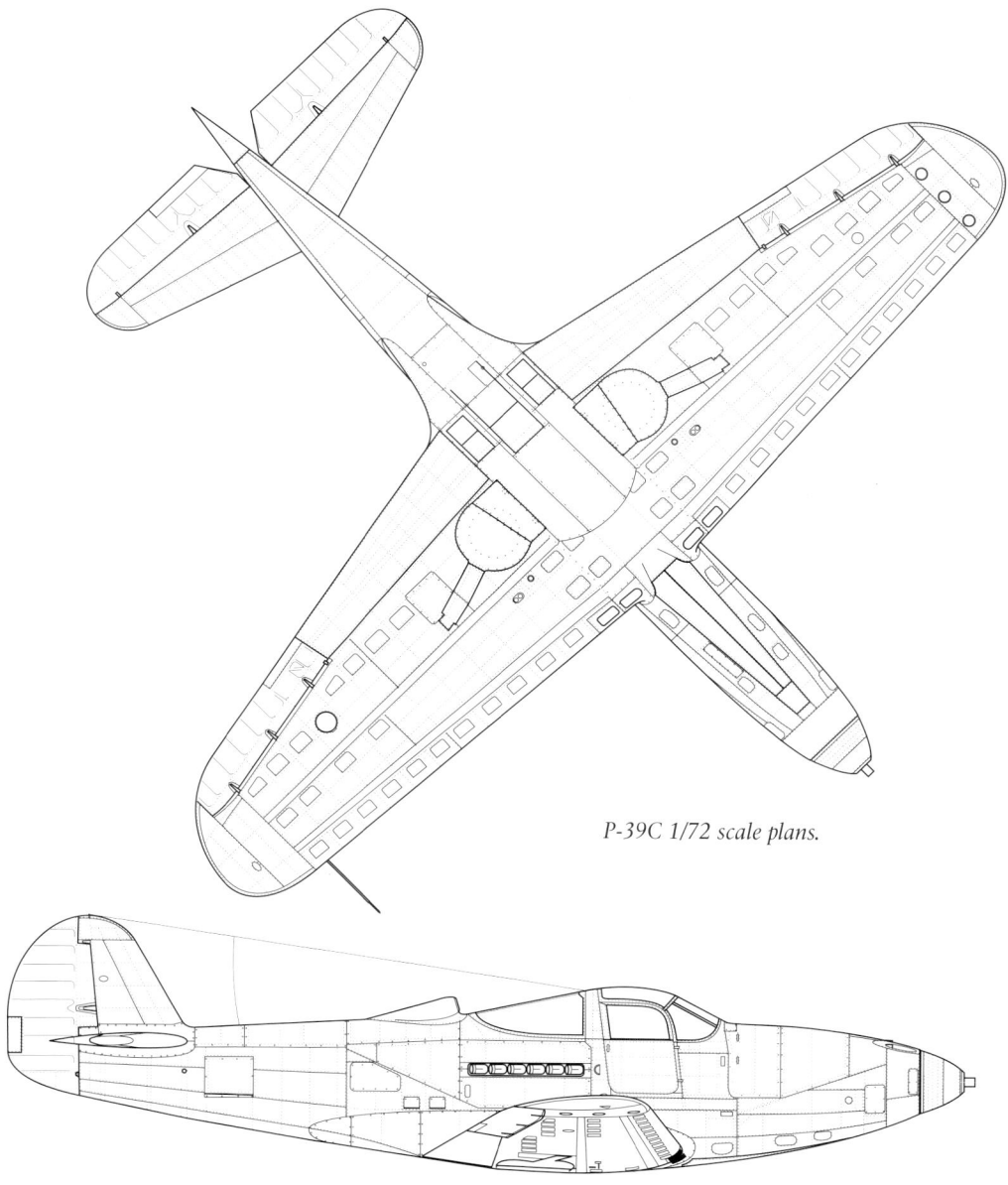

P-39C 1/72 scale plans.

Bell P-39D Airacobra

On 13 September 1940, 394 P-39Ds (Model 15) were ordered. It was the first Airacobra which could be considered as being combat-ready.

The P-39D differed from the P-39C mostly in having a better armament. It had four wing-mounted 0.30 in machine guns with 1,000 rpg, two fuselage-mounted 0.50 in machine guns with 200 rpg, plus the 37 mm cannon (with increased ammunition capacity of 30 rounds). Bulletproof windshield panels were added, and some armour protection for the pilot. Also self-sealing fuel tanks were introduced, which reduced internal fuel capacity from 141.5 Imp gal to 100 Imp gal. A 72.4 Imp gal drop tank could be carried on a rack fitted underneath the fuselage. Also a 300 lb or 600 lb bomb could be carried.

A different 10 ft 5-inch Curtiss Electric propeller was fitted. Additionally a small dorsal strake was added just ahead of the fin. The bulletproof windshield and armour protection added 245 lb to the weight of the aircraft.

P-39D Serials:
40-2991~40-3050 – 60 aircraft (converted P-39C)
41-6722~41-7115 – 394 aircraft

P-39D during test. (Stratus coll.)

P-39D side view. 1/72 scale.

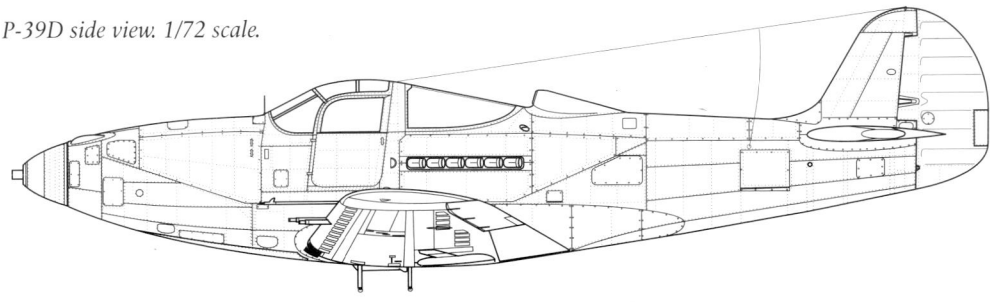

Airacobra I for the RAF, P-400

The export version of the Airacobra was known as the Bell Model 14. It was powered by a 1,150 hp Allison V-1710-35 (E4) engine which had twelve exhaust stacks on each side.

France was sufficiently interested to order 200 Model 14s on 8 October 1939, but aircraft were not delivered because of the fall of France.

In 1940, the British were desperate for combat aircraft and were willing to consider just about anything that had wings. Consequently, when Bell submitted specifications to the British Direct Purchase Commission for a fighter with a top speed of 400 mph, a ceiling of 36,000 feet, and a range of 1,000 miles, the Commission jumped in and ordered 675 Bell Model 14s sight unseen on 13 April 1940.

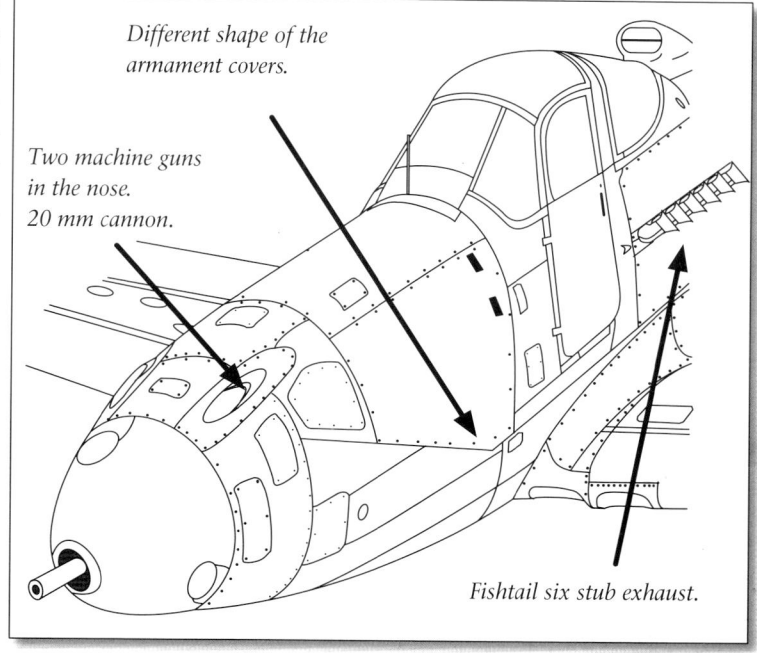

Different shape of the armament covers.
Two machine guns in the nose.
20 mm cannon.
Fishtail six stub exhaust.

The RAF model was at first named Caribou, but later the American name of Airacobra was adopted. The British Airacobra was identical to the American P-39D, but the 37-mm cannon was replaced with the faster-

P-39C, serial DS173 (ex 40-2981) one of the 3 Lend-Lease aircraft sent to the RAF. This Airacobra was used in the evaluation programme.. (Stratus coll.)

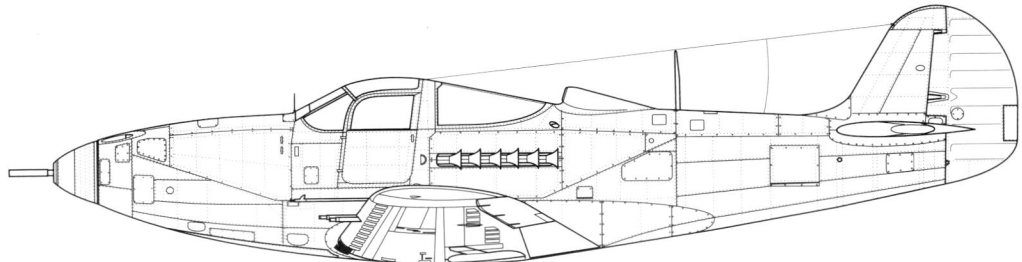

Airacobra I produced for RAF, with 6 stub exhaust. 1/72 scale plan.

Two photos of Airacobras I of 601 Squadron RAF. Only one RAF squadron ever received the Airacobra. 601 Sqn "City of London" swapped its Hurricane IICs for Airacobras in August 1941, just in time to see the aircraft withdrawn to have twenty-five modifications made to the fuselage. The first four aircraft were finally declared operational in October 1941. The Airacobra's RAF combat career lasted from 9-11 October 1941. (Flight)

firing and more reliable Hispano 20 mm cannon with 60 rounds. Two 0.50 in machine guns were mounted in the fuselage, and four 0.303 in machine guns were mounted in the wings.

The Airacobra I was powered by an Allison V-1710-35 (E4) twelve-cylinder V in-line engine rated at 1,150 hp for take-off. Only eighty of the British Airacobras were assembled for the RAF. Most of the remaining aircraft were dispatched to the Soviet Union, while the rest remained in the United States.

The British serials of the Airacobras were:
AH570~AH739 (170 planes),
AP264~AP384 (121 planes),
BW100~BW183 (84 planes),
BX135~BX434 (300 planes).
212 were sent to the USSR (54 were lost in transit)

Back to the USA

After Pearl Harbor, the USA found itself in desperate need of aircraft. Nearly 200 of the British direct-purchase Airacobras still in the USA were promptly requisitioned by the USAAC. Although they were similar to the USAAC's P-39Ds, they were not identical and were known by the USAAC under the non-standard designation of P-400. The USAAC P-400s retained their original British serial numbers and their three-colour camouflage paint. Most of these planes were used for training purposes, but some of them were rushed to the Southwest Pacific in an attempt to stem the Japanese advance. 179 of the Airacobras sent to Britain were re-acquired by the USAAF and were sent to North Africa to join the Twelfth Air Force.

P-400 with a ferry tank in England circa 1943. Aircraft, probably being prepared for USAAF use in Africa. (via P. Skulski)

P-400 with 75 US gal. drop tank. 1/72 scale.

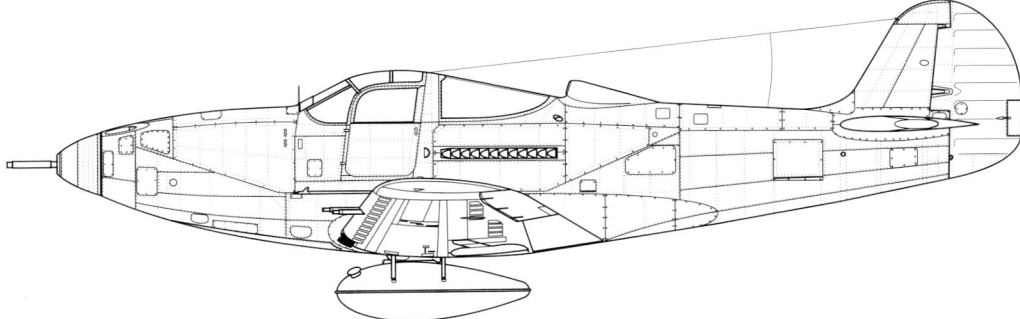

P-400 of unknown unit in New Guinea. (US National Archive)

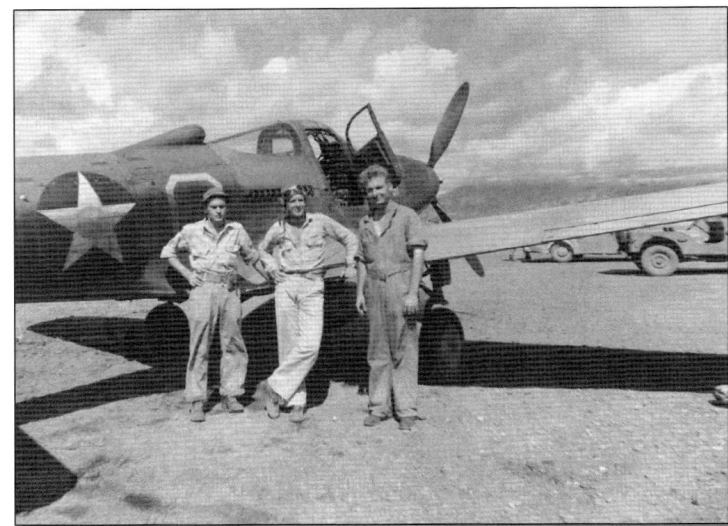

***Below**: P-400 serial BW 167, '6' of 67th Pursuit Squadron USAAF. September 1942, Henderson field, Guadalcanal. (via A. Lochte)*

P-400 nose details.

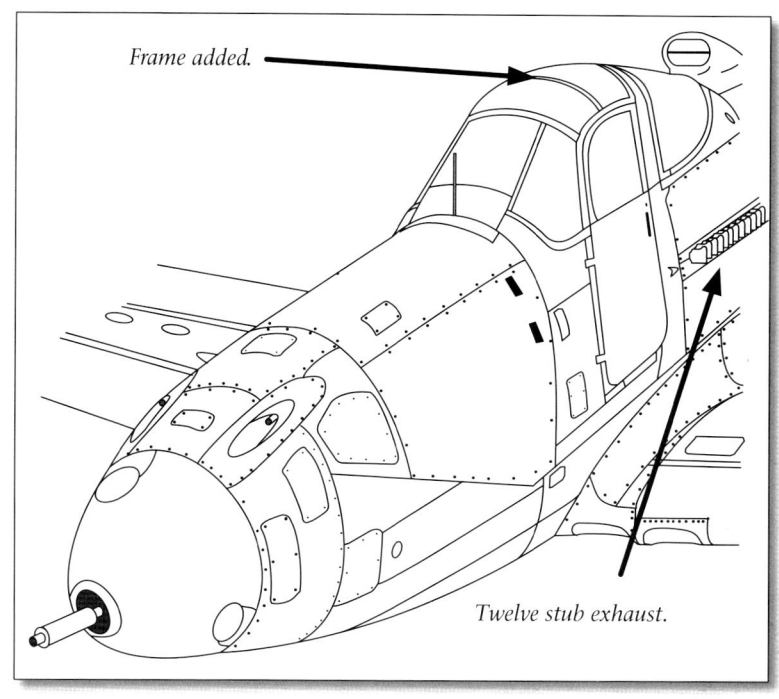

Frame added.

Twelve stub exhaust.

P-400 of an unknown unit. (US National Archive)

Bell P-39D-1 & D-2 Airacobra

P-39D-1

Further P-39D versions were ordered specifically for delivery under Lend-Lease. They were produced in two batches - P-39D-1-BE and P-39D-2-BE.

150 P-39D-1-BEs were ordered on 11 June, 1941 under contract AC 32. 185 more were ordered on 17 September 1941 under Contract AC 156.

The P-39D-1-BE (Bell Model 14A) was powered by an Allison V-1710-35 engine. Like the P-400, the P-39D-1 was armed with a 20 mm M1 cannon rather than the 37 mm Oldsmobile cannon, but the four 0.303 in wing guns of the P-400 were replaced by 0.30 in guns. The two fuselage-mounted 0.50 in machine guns were retained. A total of 336 P-39D-1s were built.

Serials:
41-28257~28406
41-38220~38404
41-38563

P-39D-1, one of the aircraft sent to Russia. Aircraft of 19 GIAP. Personal aircraft of lt. W. W. Gabriniec, spring 1942. (Stratus coll.)

P-39 D-1 serial 41-28360, '253' in flight. This aircraft crashed in Florida on 25 October 1942. (via A. Lochte)

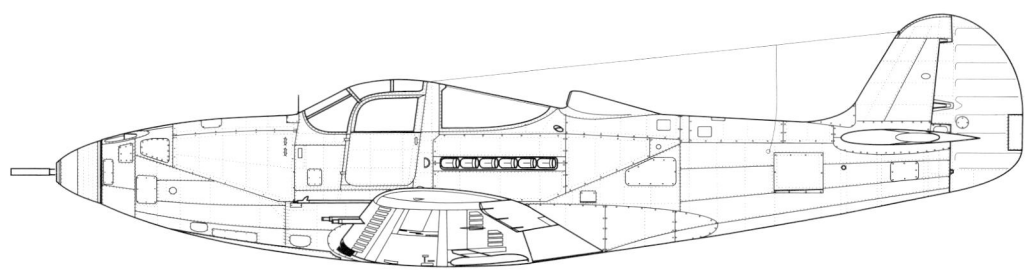

Above: *P-39D-1, side view. 1/72 scale.*
Below: *P-39D-1, serial 41-38382, No. 31 of 36th FS, 8th FG, 5th AF. Australia 1943. (US National Archive)*

Above. P-39D-1, serial 41-38343 of 5th FS 8th FG, Gurney Field Milne bay New Guinea 1943.
Below: P-39D-1, serial 41-38367, "LiL" & "Elsie" of 35th FS, 8th FG, Stephen Fields, 1943. (Both Darryl Ford)

P-39 D-2

158 aircraft on the Lend-Lease order were produced as the P-39D-2-BE (Model 14A-1). These were assembled under contract AC 156 placed on 1 June 1941. The P-39D-2s were powered by the uprated 1,325 hp V-1710-63 (E6) engine and had a 2:1 reduction gear. Aircraft was equipped with the 37 mm nose cannon. They were otherwise identical to the P-39D-1. The P-39D-2-BE could carry a 145 US gallon drop tank underneath the fuselage.

Most of these planes were originally intended for the United Kingdom. However, the Royal Air Force had rejected the Airacobra as a combat type, and most of these planes were delivered to the Soviet Union instead.

Not all of the P-39D-1 and D-2 aircraft were delivered to the Soviet Union. Several dozen were taken on charge by USAAC squadrons and were flown in combat.

Serials:
41-38405~41-38562
108 P-39D-1 & D-2 were sent to the USSR

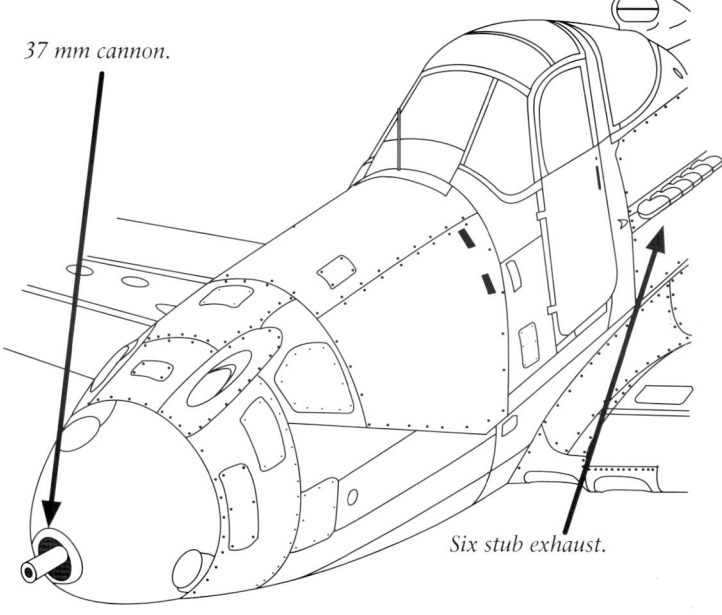

37 mm cannon.

Six stub exhaust.

P-39D-2 side elevation. 1/72 scale.

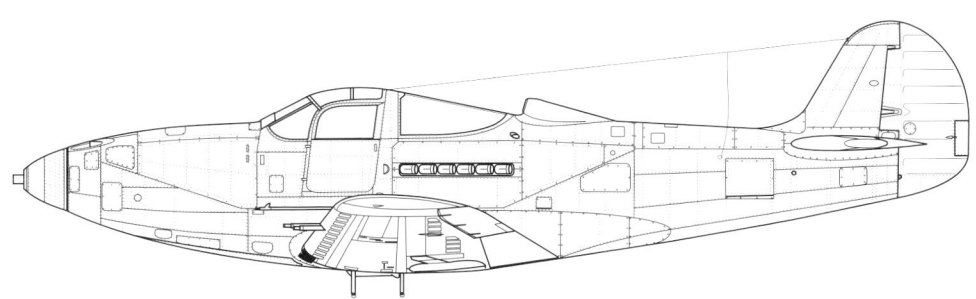

Reconnaissance version

26 P-39D aircraft were modified to P-39D-3 reconnaissance configuration. These aircraft had K-24 and K-25 cameras mounted in the rear of the fuselage. Extra armour was added to protect oil and glycol coolers from ground fire.

P-39D-3 serials:
40-3025, 41-6767, 6773, 6780, 6791, 6818, 6965, 6985, 6990, 7002, 7011, 7012, 7025, 7027, 7031, 7035, 7040, 7061, 7062, 7065, 7068, 7073, 7075, 7094,7 097

The P-39D-4-BE was the designation was given to 11 reconnaissance modifications of the P-39D-1-BE.
P-39D-4 serials: 41-28288, 38340, 28367, 28370, 28375, 28400, 28402, 38296, 38301, 38315.

Camera installation in radio bay hatch. This installation was commonly used in reconnaissance aircraft of 71st Tactical Reconnaissance group.
P-39Q-5 serial 42-19975. After this modification the aircraft was redesignated P-39Q-6.
(Stratus coll.)

Two cameras located in the lower aft part of the fuselage just behind the trailing edge of the wings.
Used in all reconnaissance versions of the P-39.
(Stratus coll.)

Bell XP-39E Airacobra

On 10 April 1941, two P-39Ds were ordered to be modified and flight tested under contract AC18373 as flying testbeds for the experimental Continental V-1430-1 supercharged inverted-Vee engine that was expected to deliver 2100 hp. These aircraft were assigned the designation XP-39E. The company designation was Model 23. A third machine was later added to the order as a non-flying static test example.

Because the Continental engine was not yet ready when the XP-39E airframes were completed, the 1325 hp Allison V-1710-47 engine was installed in its place. To receive better high-altitude performance, the V-1710-47 engine was equipped with a two-stage supercharger and an Aeroproducts propeller.

Serials:
41-19501~19502
41-71464

Bell P-39F Airacobra

The next version of the Airacobra was the P-39F (Bell Model 15B). It was almost identical to the P-39D, but had an Aeroproducts hydraulic constant-speed propeller, because the Curtiss-Electric units could not be delivered in sufficient quantities. The F also differed externally from the D in having twelve exhaust stacks on each side of the fuselage rather than six.

Initial orders, placed on September 13, 1940 under contract AC 15675, were for 229 aircraft.

The last 25 P-39Fs were fitted with the 1,100 hp V-1710-59 engine with automatic boost control and were redesignated P-39J. Serials were 41-7043~7056 and 41-7059~7079. (See P-39J)

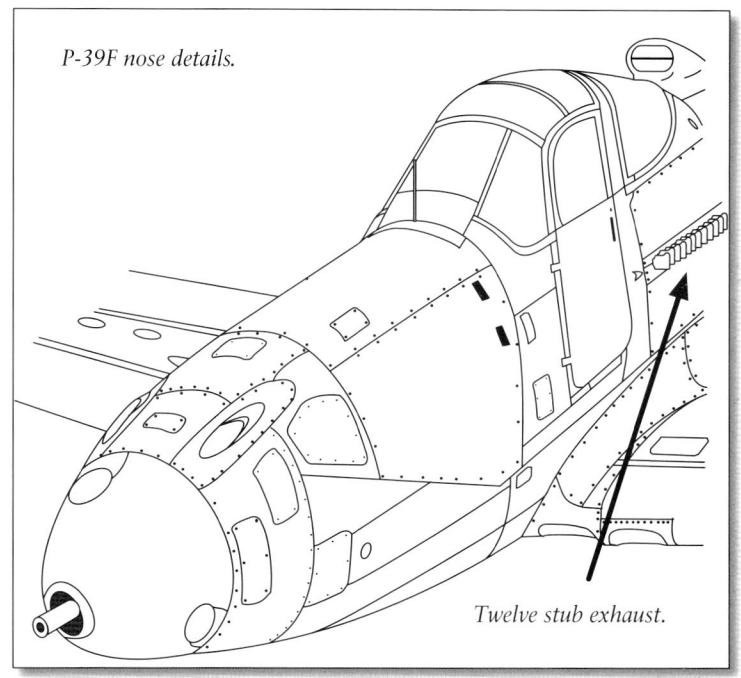

P-39F nose details.

Twelve stub exhaust.

P-39F serial 41-7341 of 56th FS, 54th FG, Nome, AK, 1942. (via. P. Skulski)

P-39F side view. 1/72 scale.

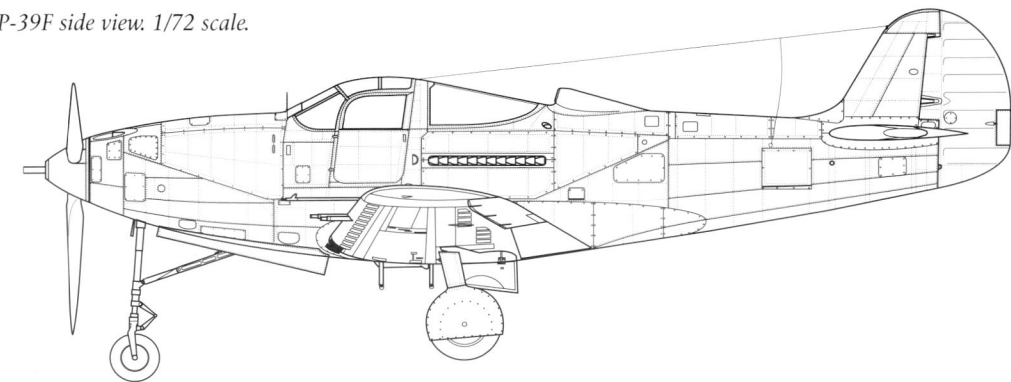

Above: P-39F serial 41-7179, '66', of 56th FS, 54th FG at Longview AB, Alaska 1942. (US National Archive)

TP-39F side view. 1/72 scale..

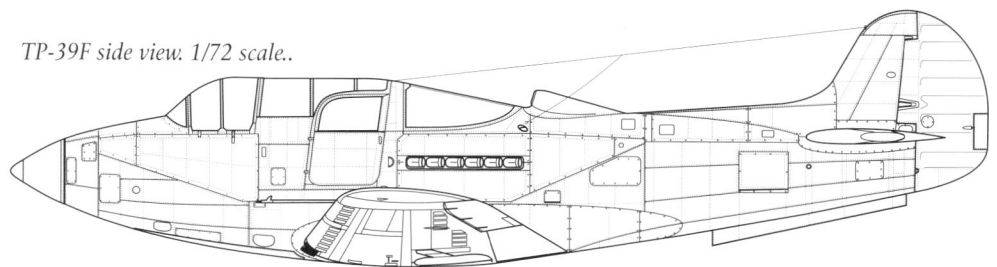

Serials:
41-7116~41-7344

27 Fs were modified in the field to become P-39F-2s (reconnaissance, ground support standard) with the addition of belly armour and the fitting of cameras to the rear fuselage, similar to the D-3.

Serials of aircraft modified as P-39F-2:

(41-) 7123, 7177, 7182, 7183, 7226, 7230, 7248, 7266, 7270, 7271, 7272, 7278, 7294, 7295, 7299, 7302, 7303, 7305, 7309, 7310, 7312, 7318, 7325, 7326, 7332, 7334, 7339.

It is known that a single P-39F was experimentally modified as a trainer with a second cockpit ahead of the original one. All armament was removed, and dual controls were fitted. The designation given to this aircraft was TP–39F.

Two photos of TP-39F during tests. (Stratus coll.)

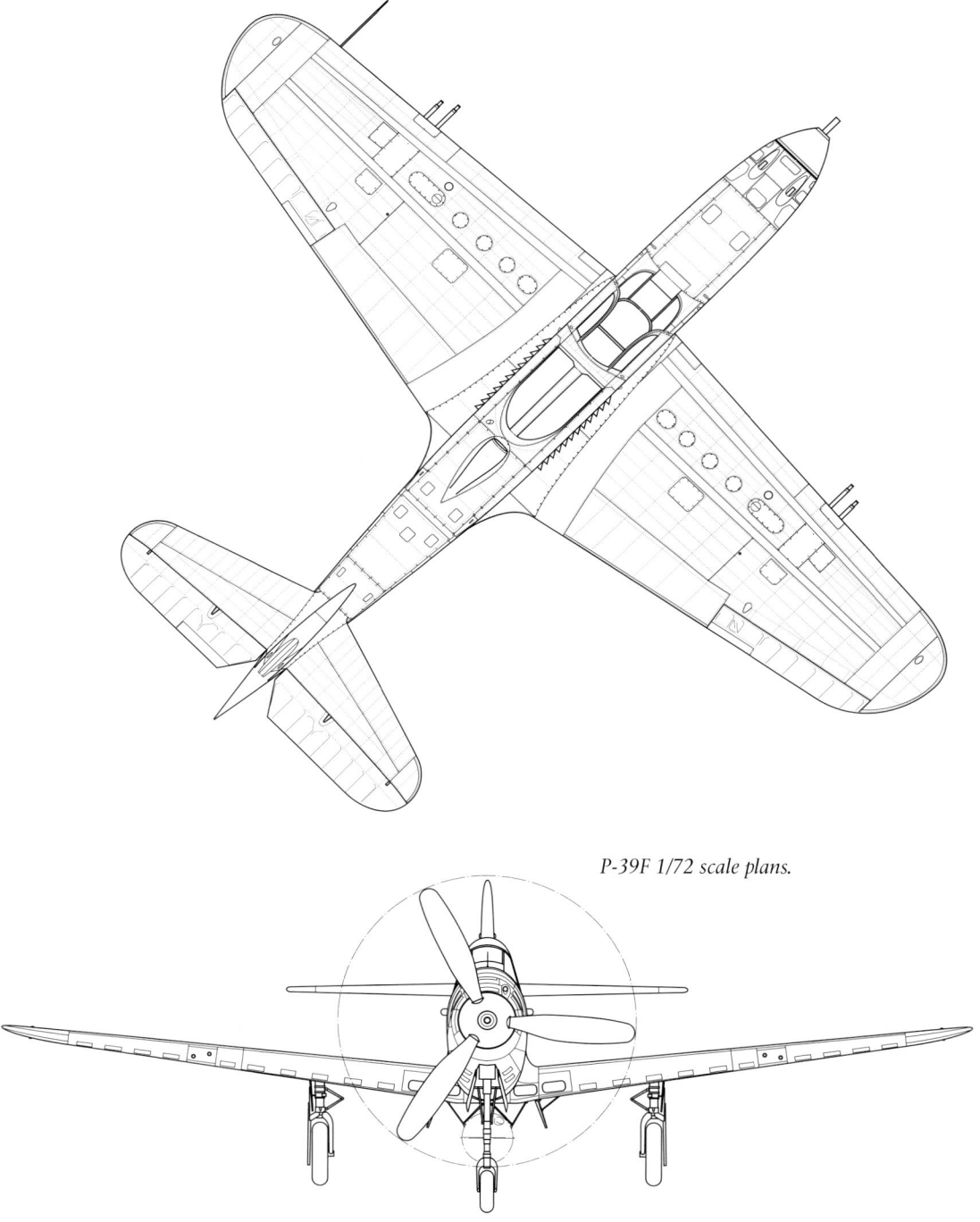

P-39F 1/72 scale plans.

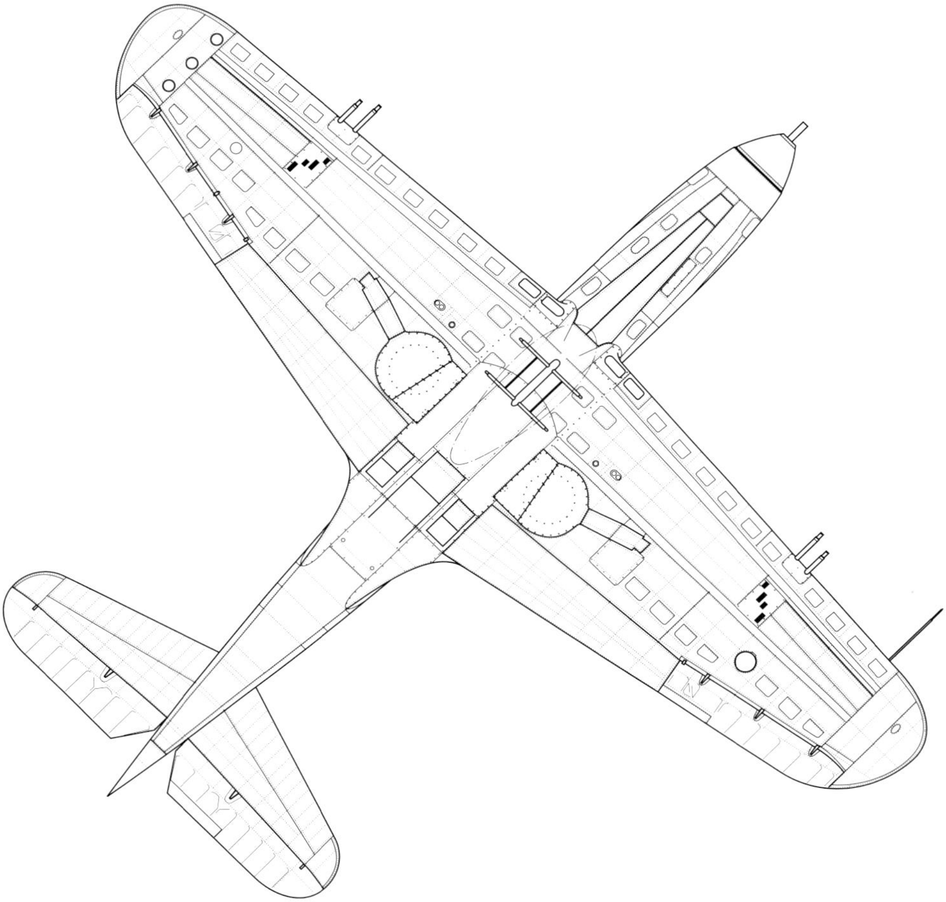

P-39F 1/72 scale plans.

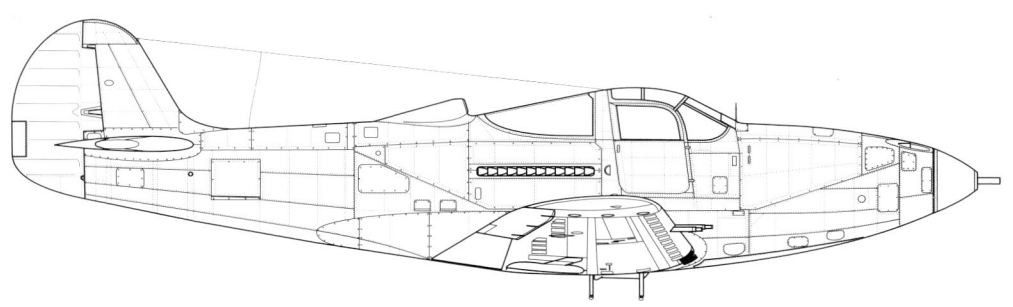

Bell P-39J Airacobra

The remaining 25 aircraft on the P-39F order were delivered as P-39Js. They had a different engine, the 1,100 hp V-1710-59 (E12) with an automatic manifold pressure regulator.

Serials:
41-7053~41-7056
42-7059~41-7079.

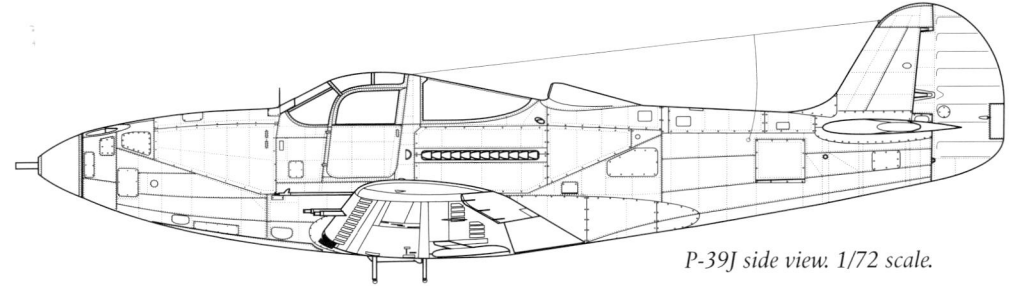

P-39J side view. 1/72 scale.

Bell P-39G/H Airacobra

These aircraft were originally intended to be identical to the P-39D-2 except for the new Aeroproducts propeller. However, the P-39G underwent several modifications during the contract stage, leading to different suffix letters being applied as production progressed, and none was actually delivered with the "G" suffix letter.

1800 P-39Gs (Bell Model 26) were ordered on 21 August 1941.
Serials were 42-4244 - 42-5043 and 42-8727 - 42-9726.

Bell P-39K Airacobra

The first of the redesignated P-39Gs were the P-39K-1-BE production lot (Model 26A). They differed from the P-39D-2 in being powered by a 1,325 hp V-1710-63 (E6) engine with an Aeroproducts propeller. 210 aircraft were ordered on 25 August 1941. The armament was the same as that of the P-39D, but the aircraft weighed 800 lb more. Also small vents were added each side of the nose.

Six P-39Ks were converted to ground attack/photo reconnaissance configuration as the P-39K-2-BE.
Serials were:
42-4244,
42-47273,
42-4352, 42-4387,
42-4433, 42-4437.

One P-39K was converted to P-39K-5-BE with a V-1710-85 (E19) engine as the prototype for the P-39N.

P-39K serials:
42-4244 - 42-4453
40 P-39Ks were sent to the USSR.

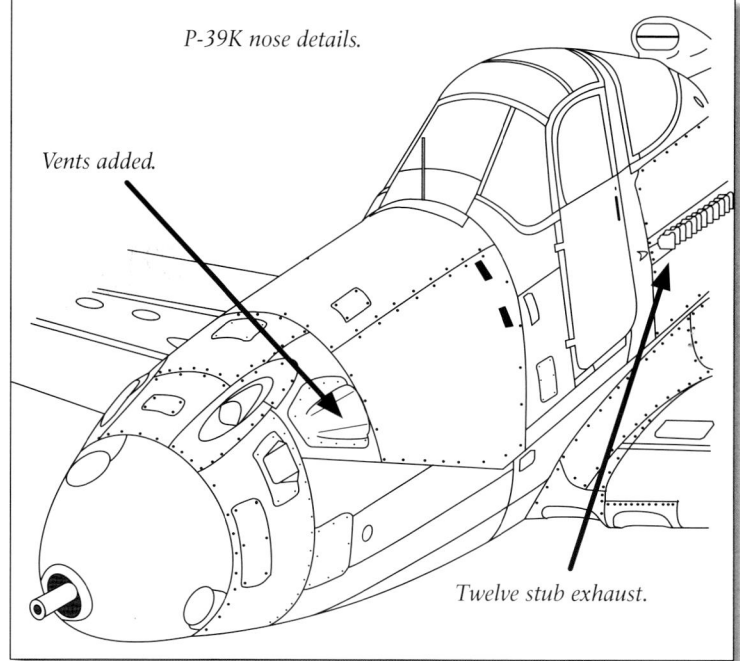

P-39K nose details. Vents added. Twelve stub exhaust.

P-39K-1 serial 42-4358, '23' of 35th FG, 40th FS, 5th AF at 12 Mile Drome, New Guinea, 1943. Pilot William McDonough (right). Groundcrew: Sgt Palzuski and Sgt Pierce. (US National Archive)

P-39K, serial 42-4383 of the training unit at Patterson Field, Oh, 1942. (US National Archive)

P-39K with "Bazooka" launchers, 1/72 scale.

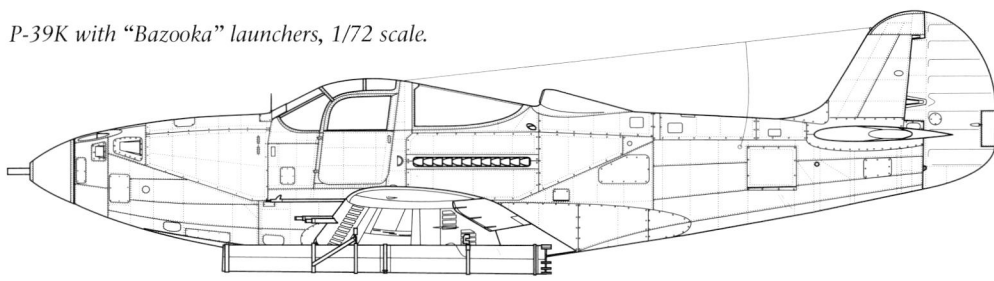

P-39K-1, serial 42-4395, Patterson Field, Fairfield, Ohio, 1944. (Stratus coll.)

Bell P-39L Airacobra

The second batch of redesignated P-39Gs were the 250 P-39Ls.

They were powered by the 1,325 hp Allison V-1710-63 engine, and differed from the K in reverting to the Curtiss Electric propeller. A new nose wheel of different design was fitted, which offered less drag at take-off. The tyre had a low-profile, smooth contour. Provision was made for the fitting of rocket rails under the wings.

Eleven were modified for photo-reconnaissance under the designation P-39L-2-BE.

The serials of these planes were 42-4457, 42-4461, 42-4462, 42-4465, 42-4466, 42-4470, 42-4471, 42-4476, 42-4489, 42-4553, and 42-4630.

P-39L serials:
42-4454 - 42-4703
137 were sent to the USSR.

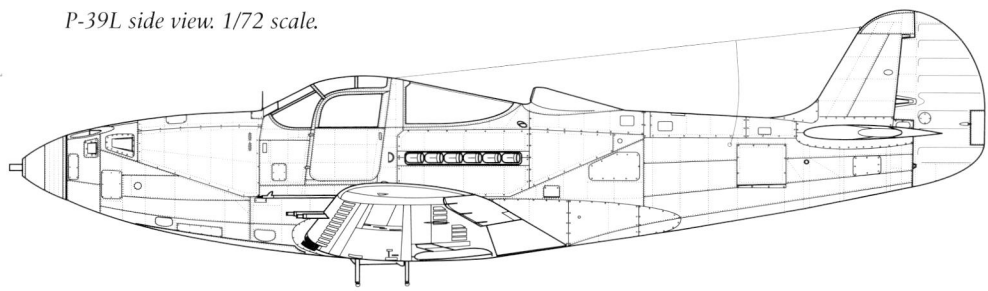

P-39L side view. 1/72 scale.

P-39L, serial 42-4558 of 93rd FG in Tunisia July, 1943. Note that aircraft still has older style nose wheel. Aircraft in non standard camouflage, but with many additions: overpainted code letters by added insignia bars. See also colour profile on page 150. (via A. Lochte)

Above: P-39L, serial 42-4460, '64' at Tonopah AAF, Nevada, 1943. (Stratus coll.)
Below: P-39L-1-BE, serial 43-4673 at Nome, Alaska, in 1942-43 during transfer to USSR. Note the low profile tyre of the nose wheel. (US National Archive)

Bell P-39M Airacobra

The third series of redesignated P-39Gs was the 240 P-39M-1-BE (Model 26D), which were ordered on 25 August 1941.

P-39Ms were equipped with an 11 ft 1 in diameter Aeroproducts propeller. They also had a new engine, the V-1710-67 (E8). This powerplant developed 1,200 hp for takeoff and 1,125 hp at 15,500 feet.

A total of 240 P-39Ms were built.

Some M-1s were fitted with the V-1710-83 (E18) engine, either as a retrofit or a change midway along the production line.

Eight P-39Ms were converted for the photographic reconnaissance role as the P-39M-2-BE. Serials were 42-4704~42-4706, 42-4710, 42-4712, 42-4751, 42-4795, 42-4824.

P-39M-1 serials:
42-4704 - 42-4943
157 were sent to the USSR

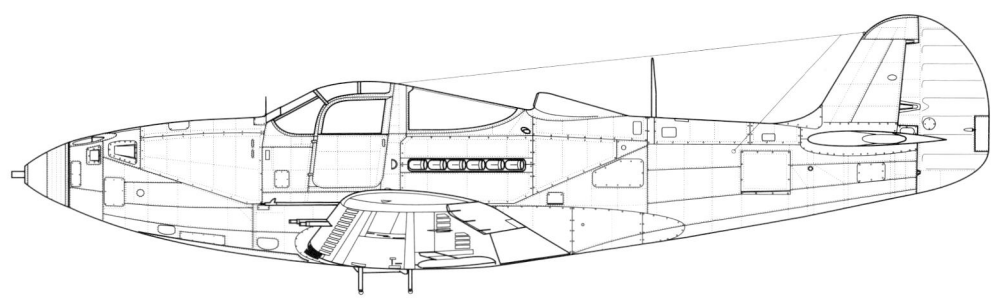

P-39M side view. 1/52 scale.

P-39M in Soviet markings photographed at Wetaskiwin, Alberta, Canada, 1942. (via T. Kopański)

P-39M of unknown unit. (via A. Lochte)

Cockpit of P-39M with switch panel to control cameras. Panel is located below and just aft of the throttle quadrant on the left side of the cockpit, almost on the floor. (Stratus coll.)

P-39N, serial 42-4961 at Nome, Alaska. US National Archive.

Bell P-39N Airacobra

The first Airacobra model to be produced in really large numbers was the P-39N (Bell Model 26C and F), 2,095 examples being built.

The first 1100 P-39Ns were part of that order for P-39Gs which had been distributed among P-39Ks, Ls, and Ms, but the rest, 995 Ns, were new orders.

All P-39Ns were powered by the V-1710-85 (E19) engine rated at 1,200 hp for take-off and 1,115 hp at 15,500 feet. The engine had a different propeller reduction gear ratio and an Aeroproducts propeller in place of the Curtiss Electric.

After completion of the first 166 P-39Ns, the USAAF ordered that four fuel cells be removed in order to reduce the internal fuel capacity from 120 to 87 US gallons, and so reduce the maximum permissible gross weight from 9,100 lbs to 8,750 lbs.

The first 166 P-39Ns were fitted with an Aeroproducts propeller having a diameter of 10 ft 4 in. Beginning with the 167th P-39N, an Aeroproducts propeller of 11 ft 7 in was used.

The 500 P-39Ns were followed by 900 P-39N-1s (Model 26C). These differed only in some minor internal changes, which altered the location of the centre of gravity.

The last Ns were the 695 P-39N-5s (Model 26C-5). They differed from earlier Ns in having the total weight of armour reduced from 231 to 193 lb. A curved armour head plate was exchanged for the bulletproof glass behind the pilot. An SCR-695 radio and a new oxygen system were fitted.

35 P-39Ns were converted to P-39N-3-BE, 128 P-39N-1-BEs to P-39N-2-BE, and 84 P-39N-5-BEs to P-39N-6-BE as ground support, reconnaissance versions.

An order for 205 additional P-39Ns was cancelled.

P-39N-5-BE, serial 42-18802 of 4th FS, 35th FG at base-Tsili Tsili, August 1943. Personal aircraft of Lt. Roy Owen. (via P. Skulski)

Serials	Subversion	Quantity
42-4944~42-5043	Bell P-39N-BE originally part of P-39G order.	100
42-8727~42-9126	Bell P-39N-BE originally part of P-39G order.	400
42-8808~42- 8842	Converted to P-39N-3-BE	
42-9127~42-9726	Bell P-39N-1-BE originally part of P-39G order.	600
9141,9145, 9148,9150,9152,9211,9255,9416,9615,9677,9697~9712, 9714~9724,9726	Converted to P-39N-2.	
42-18246~42-18545	Bell P-39N-1-BE	300
18276~18285,18287~18296,18298~18300,18302~18305,18310, 18327,18466,18485~18546	Converted to P-39N-2	
42-18546~42-19240	Bell P-39N-5-BE	695
18676~18681,18712~18725,18768,18818,18829,18831,18841,18857,18870,18876~18879,18881,18882,18884,18887, 18889~18896,18899~18907,18909~18921,18923~18925, 18927~18933,18935~18941,18947,19043	Converted to P-39N-6.	
42-19241~42-19445	Cancelled contract for Bell P-39N Airacobra	

1113 of P-39N were exported to USSR.

P-39N, '51' (?) of unknown unit. (via T. Kopański)

P-39N with 500 lb bomb. 1/72 scale.

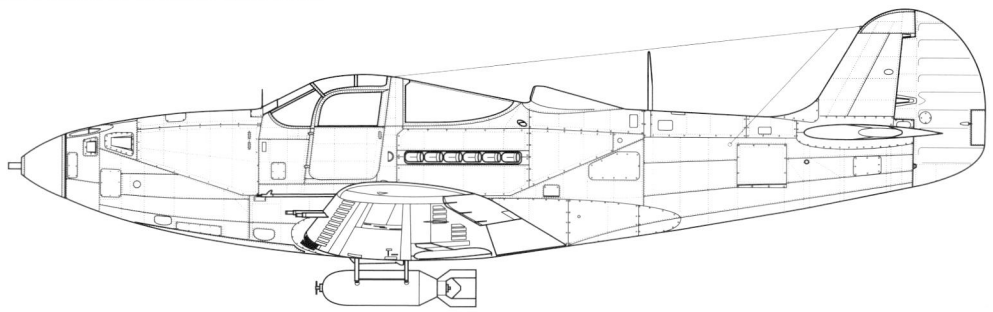

P-39N (Soviet) without wing guns and with RPK-10, (RahdioPoluKompas - direction finder) under rear fuselage. 1/72 scale.

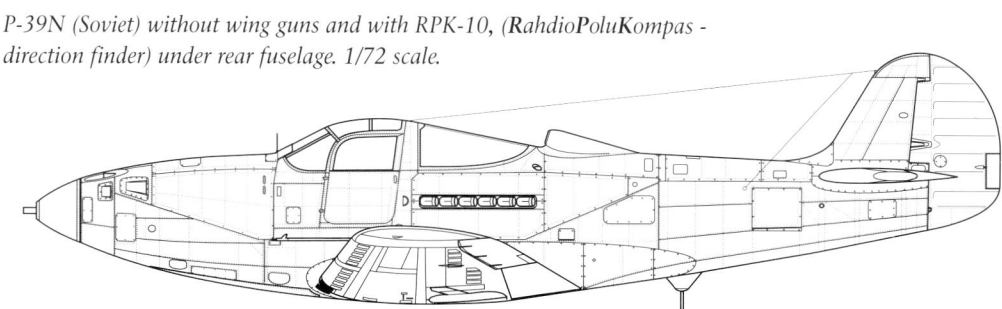

P-39N, serial 42-8748 during delivery to Russia. (Stratus coll.)

Bell P-39Q Airacobra

The P-39Q was the last production version of the Airacobra. It was also the version which was built in the largest numbers, 4,905 P-39Qs being built before production ended.

The principal difference between the P-39Q and earlier versions was in the fighter's armament - the four wing-mounted 0.30 in machine guns were replaced by two 0.50 in machine guns mounted in fairings underneath each wing. The ammunition capacity of the underwing guns was 300 rpg. The two fuselage-mounted 0.50 in machine guns with 200 rpg, plus the hub-mounted 37 mm cannon with 30 rounds, were retained.

The engine was the Allison V-1710-85 (E19) of 1,200 hp, the same powerplant that was used in the P-39N.

There were several production blocks of the P-39Q:

P-39Q-1-BE: Retained the 72.4 Imp gallon fuel capacity of the P-39N-5 but returned to the original 231 lb of armour of the P-39N-1.

P-39Q-2-BE: Five Q-1s were modified to carry cameras for photographic reconnaissance by adding K-24 and K-25 cameras in the aft fuselage.

P-39Q-5-BE (Model 26Q-5): Reverted to the lighter armour fit of the P-39N-5 (193.4 lb), as well as the use of the full wing fuel capacity (92.6 Imp gall) characteristic of the P-39M. Type A-1 bombsight adapters were added to the P-39Q-5-BEs at the Modification Centre before delivery to operational units.

P-39Q-6-BE: 148 Q-5s were modified to carry cameras for photographic reconnaissance by adding K-24 and K-25 cameras in the aft fuselage.

P-39Q-5, serial 42-20381 of 7th AF piloted by John M. Maxwell. (US National Archive)

P-39Q-10, serial 42-20581 in Soviet markings. This aircraft is fitted with the long-range external fuel tank. (Stratus coll.)

P-39Q-10-BE (Model 26Q-10): Internal fuel capacity rose to 100 Imp gallons and armour weight went to 227.1 lb. The throttle was linked to the propeller settings to provide automatic adjustments. There was additional winterization of the oil system, and rubber engine mounts were installed. The first P-39Q-10-BEs were delivered to the USAAF by the end of July 1943. A total of 705 examples were built, but 995 more that were assigned serial numbers 42-21251 - 22245 and actually completed as P-63E-1 Kingcobras.

P-39Q-11-BE: Eight Q-10s were modified to carry cameras for photographic reconnaissance by adding K-24 and K-25 cameras in the aft fuselage.

P-39Q-15-BE (Model 26Q-15): Differed from the Q-10 in minor equipment variations. Among these was a reinforced inclined deck to prevent the 0.50 in machine gun tripod mounting cracking, bulkhead reinforcements to prevent rudder pedal wall cracking, a reinforced reduction gearbox bulkhead to prevent cowling former cracking, and repositioning of the battery solenoid. This version was delivered beginning in August 1943. 1,000 examples were built.

P-39Q-20-BE (Model 26Q-20): The underwing 0.50 in machine gun pods were sometimes not mounted in this version. New nose wheel hub was introduced.

P-39Q-21-BE: Similar to P-39Q-20, but a four-bladed Aeroproducts propeller was fitted.

P-39Q-25-BE (Model 26Q-25): Similar to the Q-21 but with a reinforced aft-fuselage and horizontal stabilizer structure and a four-bladed Aeroproducts propeller. The wing guns were deleted from these aircraft, which were all exported to the Soviet Union. 700 were built.

P-39Q-30-BE: Tests indicated that the four-bladed propeller materially worsened directional stability, and this version reverted to the three-bladed unit. This was the last production version of the P-39Q.

On July 25, 1944, all P-39 production ceased, with 9,558 examples having been produced.

A few P-39Qs were modified into two-seaters with dual controls for use as advanced trainers, under the designation RP-39Q (redesignated TP-39Q after 1944). All armament was removed.

The first example, converted from P-39Q-5 42-20024, was rolled out for the first time on September 16, 1943. It was designated TP-39Q-5. Twelve two-seat fighter trainers were converted from P-39Q-20s, and were designated RP-39Q-22. The ventral strake was somewhat different in shape from that of the ventral fin of the original TP-39Q-5.

Serials of P-39Q Airacobra:

Serials	Subversion	Number built
42-19446~42-19595	Bell P-39Q-1	150
42-19479~42-19483	Converted to P-39Q-2-BE.	
42-19596~42-20545	Bell P-39Q-5	950
19608, 19610, 19612, 19614, 19616, 19624, 19626, 19628, 19636, 19640, 19642, 19644~19646, all even numbers 19648~19719, all odd numbers 19697~19719, 19723,19725, odd numbers 19927~19975,19977~19979, 19981, 19983, 19985, 19987, all odd numbers19989~20011, 20013~20015, 20017~20019, odd numbers 20021~20065, 20067~20069, odd numbers 20071~10092, 20095~20097, 20099, 20101, 20103, 20105	Converted to P-39Q-6-BE	
42-20546~42-21250	Bell P-39Q-10	705
44-2001~44-3000	Bell P-39Q-15	1000
44-3001~44-3850, 44-3859~44-3860, 44-3865~44-3870, 44-3875~44-3880, 44-3885~44-3890, 44-3895~44-3900, 44-44-3905~44-3910, 44-3915~44-3919, 44-3937~44-3940,	Bell P-39Q-20	885
44-3851~44-3858, 44-3861~44-3864, 44-3871~44-3874, 44-3881~44-3884, 44-3891~44-3894, 44-3901~44-3904, 44-3911~44-3914, 44-3920~44-3936, 44-3941~44-4000	Bell P-39Q-21	109
44-32167~44-32666, 44-70905~44-71104	Bell P-39Q-25	500
44-71105~44-71504	Bell P-39Q-30	400
44-3879, 3885~3887, 3889, 3895, 3897, 3905, 3906, 3908, 3917, and 3918.	RP-39Q-22	

3291 of all P-39Q were sent to USRR.

P-39Q-20, '20', "Maxine". (Stratus coll.)

P-39Q-20, serial 44-3569 of the 71st TRG, 82nd TRS. Personal aircraft of 1st Lt. Carl T. Bailey, 1944. Note redesigned nose wheel hub. (via A. Lochte)

P-39Q-1, serial 42-19549, "Tarawa Boom De-Ay" of the 318th FG, Oahu, Hawaii. (US National Archive)

P-39Q, side view (early production series), 1/72 scale..

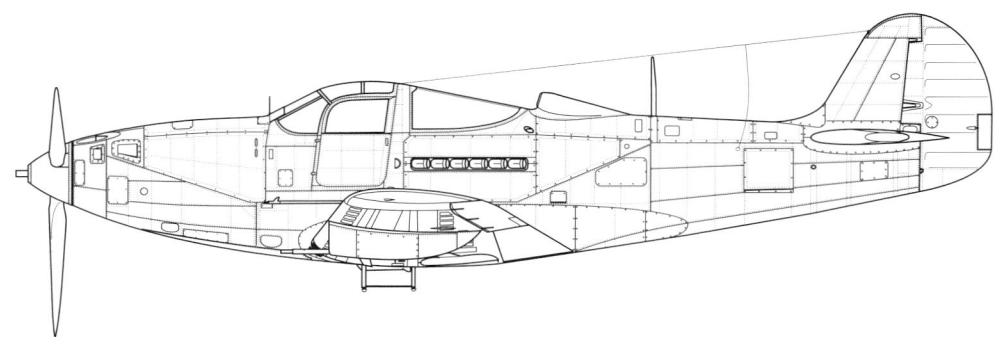

P-39Q-21, side view. 1/72 scale.

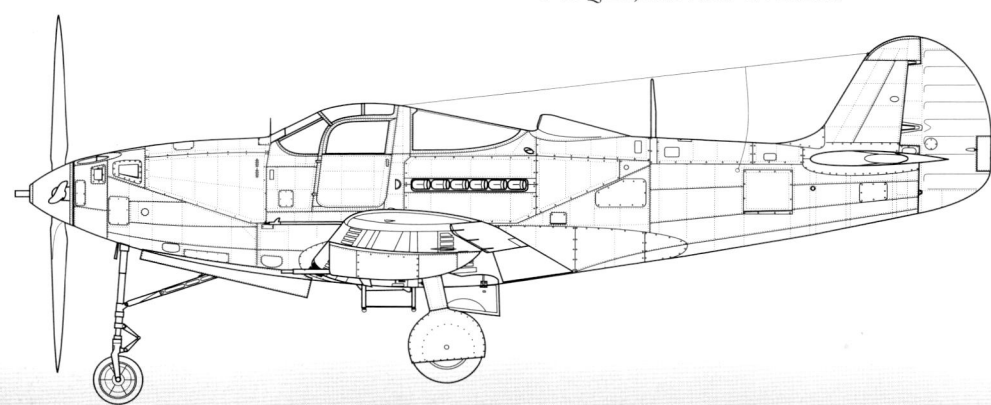

Two P-39Qs taking off at one of the Pacific island. (US National Archive)

P-39Q at Bougainville, Solomon Islands. (US National Archive)

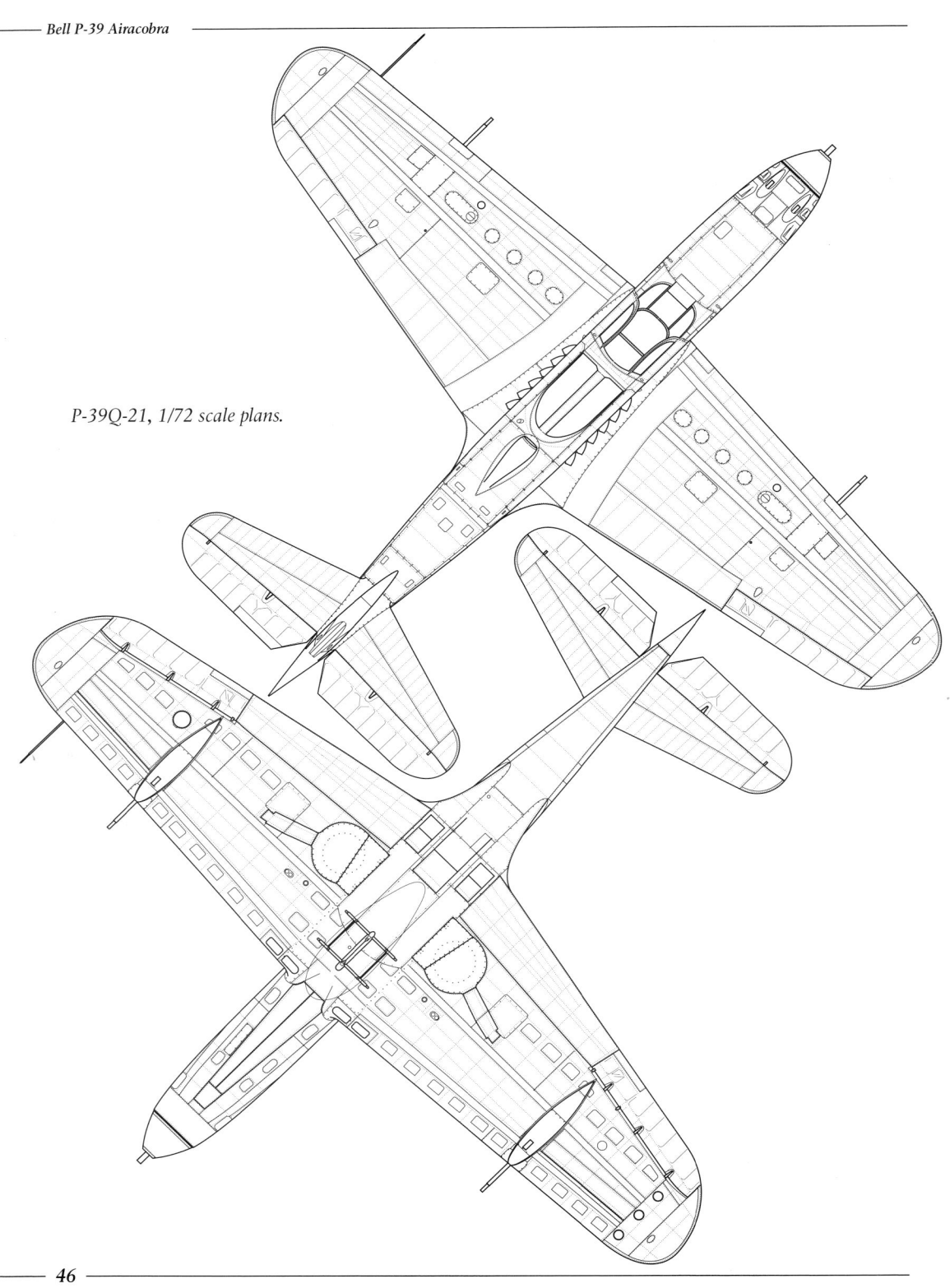

P-39Q-21, 1/72 scale plans.

P-39Q-21. 1/72 scale.

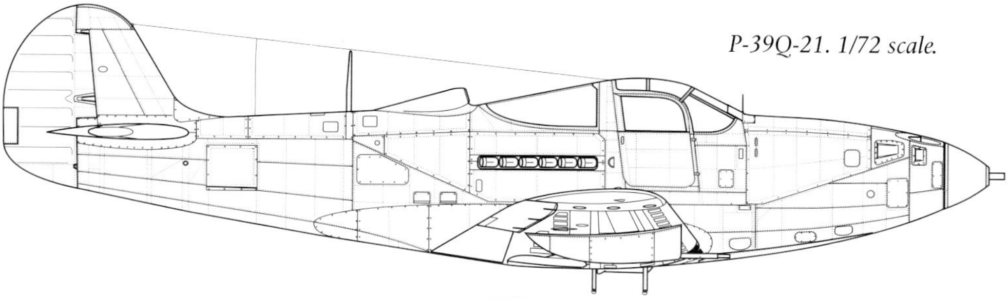

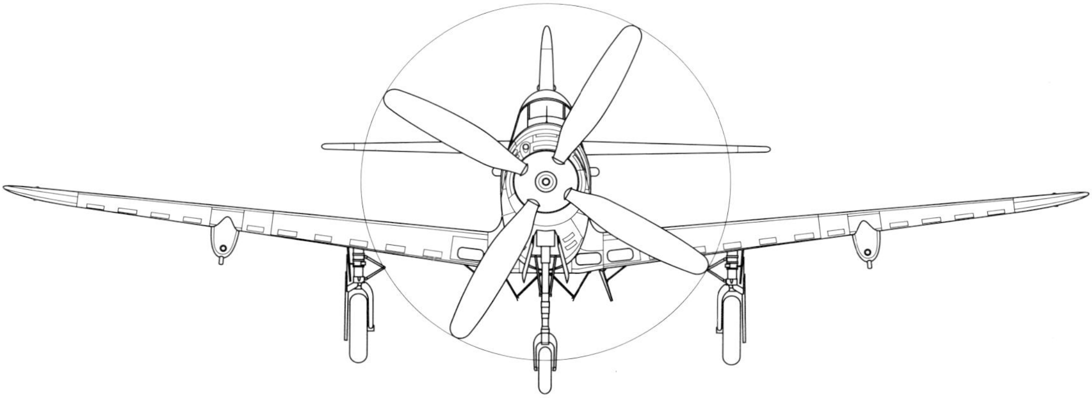

P-39Q without underwing gun pods. 1/72 scale.

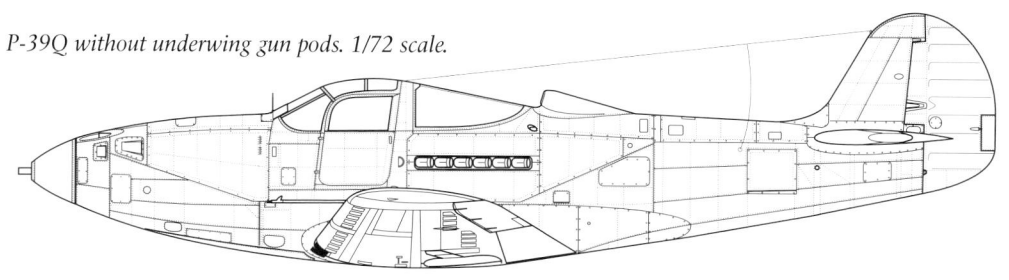

TP-39Q, side view. 1/72 scale.

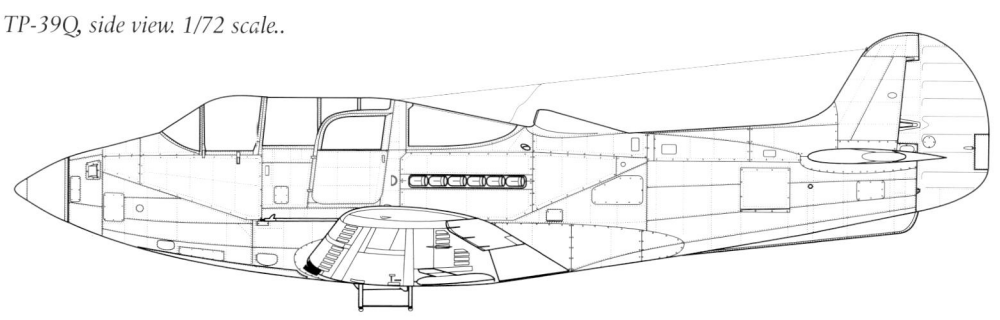

Soviet "improvements" and operating instructions.

During operation of the aeroplane in the Soviet Air Force, a number of structural problems came to light, and these were then subject to modifications made in repair workshops.

Many of these problems were subjects of detailed procedures on necessary modifications. Tests on typical problems were carried out at the CAGI (Central Aero- and Hydrodynamics Institute) which prepared the procedures for repair workshops.

Typical defects and modifications:
1. Twisting of the rear fuselage and skin deformation.

On all P-39 aircraft up to and including model Q-21 the rear fuselage has to be reinforced according to CAGI instructions:
a. fit two plates on fuselage sides around the radio compartment hatches;
b. fit rear fuselage longeron reinforcing members;
c. add two supports to forward tailplane spar attachment joints;
d. fit two plates to reinforce the port forward fuselage beam.

Additionally, in all aircraft up to model Q-30 another reinforcement of the rear fuselage has to be made should there be skin deformation.

This additional reinforcement should also be made on all aircraft used for training, regardless of model.

2. Deformation and shifting of the tail

On all aircraft, up to and including model Q-21 the tailplane should be reinforced according to CAGI instructions:
a. two duralumin plates (on top and bottom) on flanges of the forward tailplane spar, these are added on the external surface of the tailplane skin;
b. an additional plate on the spar in the fin cut-out area;
c. additional duralumin profiles fitted to the rear tailplane spar;
d. additional reinforcements of the rear tailplane spar;
e. two forward longerons should be replaced with larger cross-section profiles;
f. reinforcement of the middle elevator actuators;
g. replacement of the elevator hinges with larger ones.

On all aircraft the fin should be reinforced according to CAGI instructions:
a. reinforce the fin leading edge with additional skin;
b. add another (third) fin-fuselage attachment point;

TP-39 UTI (Soviet conversion). 1/72 scale.

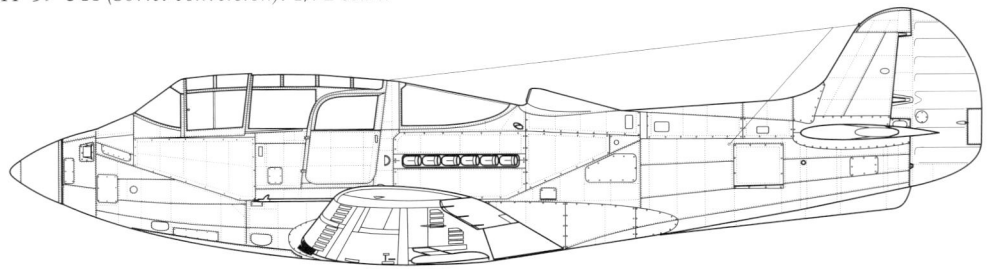

c. reinforce the forward and rear post with additional profiles;
d. additional plates at the middle rudder hinge.

As an additional precaution, in order to prevent failures many operational limitations were imposed on the aeroplane, including:
a. dive speed limit;
b. rudder deflection limit;
c. preventing "hard landings" with a highly loaded aeroplane.

Additional notes:
In order to reduce the effect of centre of gravity travel during flight a ballast of 21 to 71 kg, depending on the model and radio equipment, should be fitted forward of the battery.

It is strictly forbidden to take on board any items that are not part of the aeroplane's combat equipment. Moreover, depending on the model and radio equipment, the following armour should be removed:
a. up to model Q-5: armour aft of the oil tank;
b. in models Q-10, Q-15, Q-20, Q-21, Q-25, and Q-30: armour aft of the oil tank, three armour plates aft of the carburettor, and two duralumin plates on the sides of the carburettor.

Also, three radio equipment standards were developed for the Airacobra:
1. Basic: WS-454A receiver, BC-457A transmitter, and MN-26M(U) radio direction finder;
2. For aircraft without the radio direction finder: WS-454A receiver, BC-457A transmitter;
3. Temporary, permitted only until replaced by the basic one: WS-454A receiver and MN-26M(U) radio direction finder.

All this was developed in order to improve the position of the aeroplane's centre of gravity.

One of the Russian P-39 photographed during USAAF operations from Soviet airfields, 1944. (US National Archive)

Official USAAF P-39 Performance Figures

Model	Dimensions	Guns	Rounds per gun	Bombs	Weight (Lbs.)	High speed	Range (miles)
P-39D	Span 34'0" Length 30'2" Height 11'10" Tread 11'4" Wing area 213 sq.ft.	4 - .30 cal. 2 - .50 cal. 1 - 37 mm.	1,000 max; 300 200 30	1 – 100-500 lb.	6300 basic 7650 combat	324 mph/25,000 348 mph/20,000 360 mph/15,000 355 mph/10,000 335 mph/5,000	8850/0/295/1100* 8800/0/276/1050 8150/0/195/800 7650/0/120/600 8150/500/120/450
P-39D-1	Span 34'0" Length 30'2" Height 11'10" Tread 11'4" Wing area 213 sq.ft.	4 - .30 cal. 2 - .50 cal. 1 – 20 mm.	1,000 max; 300 200 60	As above	As above	As above	As above
P-39D-2	As above	As above	As above	As above	As above	As above	As above
P-39F	As above	4 - .30 cal. 2 - .50 cal. 1 – 37mm	1,000 max; 300 200 30	As above	As above	As above	As above
P-39K-1	As above	As above	As above	As above	As above	As above	As above
P-39L-1	As above	As above	As above	As above	6500 basic 7900 combat	323 mph/25,000 347 mph/20,000 360 mph/15,000 354 mph/10,000 335 mph/5,000	9100/0/295/1075 8400/0/195/750 7900/0/120/550 8400/500/120/400
P-39M-1	As above	As above	As above	As above	As above	357 mph/25,000 365 mph/20,000 370 mph/15,000 350 mph/10,000 330 mph/5,000	As above
P-39N (0-5)	Span 34'0" Length 30'2" Height 12'5" Tread 11'4" Wing area 213.22 sq.ft.	As above	As above	As above	6400 basic 7600 combat	368 mph/25,000 375 mph/20,000 376 mph/15,000 357 mph/10,000 330 mph/5,000	8750/0/262/975 8600/0/243/900 8050/0/162/625 7550/0/87/350 8050/500/87/275
P-39Q-1	As above	2 - .50 cal. W 2 - .50 cal. N 1 – 37mm	300 200 30	As above	As above	As above	As above
P-39Q-5	As above	As above	As above	As above	As above	As above	8900/0/285/1075 8800/0/266/1000 8200/0/185/725 7700/0/110/525 8200/500/110/375
P-39Q (10-15)	As above	As above	As above	As above	As above	As above	8950/0/295/1100 8850/0/276/1050 8250/0/195/750 7750/0/120/575 8250/500/120/425
P-39Q (20-30)	As above	As above (some P-39Qs deleted wing guns)	As above	As above	As above	As above	As above

* As follow – take off weight/bombs (lbs.)/fuel gallons/max range at 10,000 feet
Fuel tanks (integral)
120 American gallons – versions D-2, K-1, L-1, M-1, Q-10, Q-15, Q-20, Q-21, Q-25, Q-30
87 American gallons – versions N-0, N-1, N-5
110 American gallons – versions Q-5

Detailed P-39D specification according to Russian tests

Length without gun	- 9.195 m
Length with gun	- 9.580 m
Wing span	- 10.363 m
Horizontal stab. Span	- 3.962 m
Average fuselage dim.	
Height	- 1.740 m
Width	- 0.900 m
Wing dihedral	- 5° 37'
Wing sweep-back	- 4° 35'
Angle of attack. wing	- 2.5°
Angle of attack. horizontal stab.	- 2° 10'
Wheel base	- 3.040 m
Wing area	- 19.88 sq. meters
Horizontal stabiliser area	- 3.79 sq. meters.
Vertical stabiliser area	- 1.733 sq. meters
Max power of Allison V-1710-35	- 1150 hp.
Prop dia.	- 3.160 m
Weight (empty)	- 2642 kg
Weight basic	- 3556 kg
Max speed	
At sea level	- 493 km/h
At 4200 m.	- 585 km/h
Landing speed	- 145 km/h
Operational ceiling	- 9600 m
Time to reach 5000 m.	- 6.5 min.
Climb rate	
At see level	- 14.4 m/s
At 5000 m.	- 9.5 m/s

P-39 captured by the Germans in Africa. (via T. Kopański)

Combat range with 10% emergency fuel capacity at 550 m level – 993 km.

Max flight time	- 3h 45min
360° turn time	- 19 s
Take off	- 300 m
Landing	- 350 m

Aircraft tests in USSR

Aircraft	Hurricane Mk II	P-40C	P-40E	Spitfire Mk VB	P-39D-2	P-63A	Spitfire Mk IX
Tests data	Nov 1941	Oct 1941	June 1942	June 1943	April 1942	1944	Nov 1944
Engine Take off power Hp	Merlin XX	Allison V-1710-33	Allison V-1710-39	Rolls-Royce Merlin 46	Allison V-1710-35	Allison V-1710-93	Rolls-Royce Merlin 66
	1280	1055	1150	1115	1135	1325	1325
Weight (basic) kg	3170	3390	3840	2920	3556	3738	3292
Max speed km/h							
at see level	427	445	450 470*	480	472 493*	483 514*	494 528*
at altitude (m)	522	545	549 575*	578	557 585*	612 620*	614 628*
	5500	4860	4600 4750	6700	3950 4200	8600 7250	6600 6500
Time to reach 5000 m (min)	7.2	7.0	7.8	7.1	6.4	7.6 5.9*	4.4 4.0*
Full turn time at 1000 m in s.	19-20	18	19.2		17.7-18.7	20.5	17.5
Armament							
Cannon				2 x 20 mm	1 x 20 mm	1 x 37 mm	2 x 20 mm
Machine Guns	8 x 7.7 mm	2 x 12.7 mm 4 x 7.62 mm	6 x 12.7 mm	4 x 7.7 mm	2 x 12.7 mm 2 x 7.62 mm	2 x 12.7 mm	4 x 7.7 mm

P-39Q in Polish markings. Personal aircraft of the PAF commander gen. Polynin, late 1945. (via A. Glass)

Technical description

Based on the article published in Aviation magazine, May 1943.

Fuselage

The fuselage is comprised of two spliced sections known as the "forward" and "aft" fuselages.

The forward section is the structural focal point of the Airacobra and where its design philosophy takes concrete shape.

Integrally it comprises the major portion of the whole fuselage and contains the center wing section, engine bed, extension shaft and propeller gear reduction assembly mount, principal armament mounts, nose wheel attachment fittings, and supports and brackets for myriad engine accessories: fuel, lubricating, oxygen, ventilating, control, electrical and hydraulic assemblies. To it are fastened the outer wings, pilot's cabin, engine and accessories, extension shaft and reduction gear box, heavier armament and ammunition magazines, oil and Prestone cooling systems, nose wheel assembly, and aft fuselage.

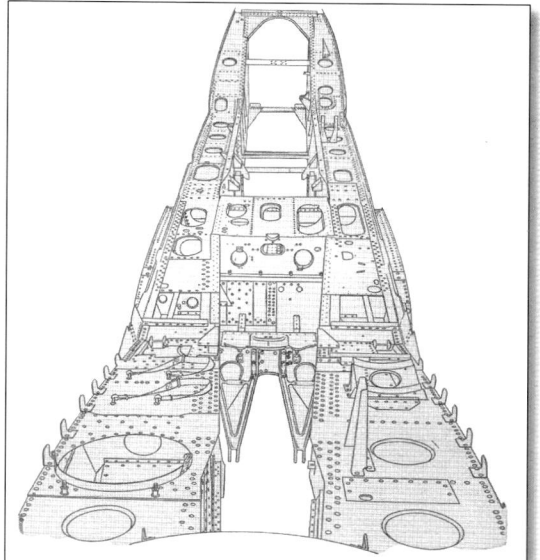

A section consists of two built-up longitudinal beams which are cradle shape in profile. Each beam is made of extruded aluminium alloy angle sections tied with solid, heavily reinforced aluminium webbing. Outboard shape is imparted through a series of forged aluminium bulkheads. A heavy gauge stamped aluminium deck plate is riveted to the tops of these bulkheads and extends the full length of the beam. To the rear of the beam is a sturdy forged angle member mounted to form the engine bed.

The outer skin of the forward fuselage consist of formed aluminium sheet riveted to the bulkheads. Skin panels in the nose section and beneath the pilot's cabin are .051 gauge, and the rear panels are .032-gauge sheet.

The two main longitudinal beams are maintained rigidly parallel as a self-contained unit, principally by tubular spreader bars, a forward bulkhead and former

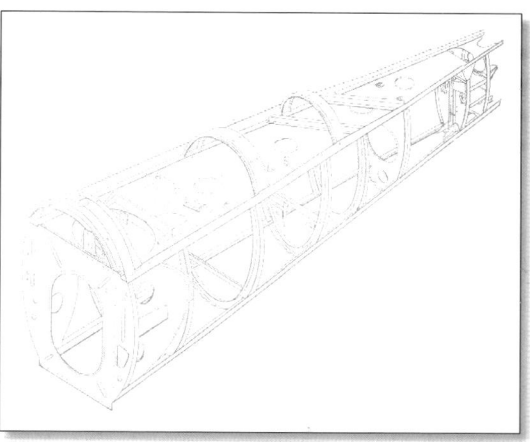

member, and the aft splicing bulkhead. The center wing section, coolant radiator supports, and pilot cabin which is joined later, also act as tieing members.

The pilot's cabin is superimposed on the forward fuselage but is designed and attached as an integral part of the fuselage just forward of the engine compartment. Fume-tight bulkheads are provided between the engine compartment and cabin and between the cabin and the armament compartment forward.

The aft fuselage section supports the complete empennage assembly and contains the radio installation. It is of ordinary semi-monocoque construction with eight principal forming bulkheads. The splicing bulkhead has a beaded sheet web and a number of drilled stiffeners for bolts joining the aft and forward fuselages. The two forward bulkheads are tied outboard by two longitudinal bulkheads to form a compartment for the engine oil tank. The skin is .032-gauge formed aluminium sheet which is flush riveted throughout.

The cowling is attached to the fuselage at four main points: the gun compartment forward of the pilot's cabin, engine compartment, the Prestone and oil radiator compartments on the underside of the wing center section, and the oil tank compartment in the aft fuselage behind the engine accessories bay.

Cowlings are formed aluminium sheet ranging from .051 gauge at the gun, Prestone and oil radiator compartments to .032 gauge at the engine and oil tank compartments.

Gun compartment cowl sections are attached to removable channel-shaped formers and bulkheads with flush-type fasteners. Engine compartment sections are strengthened with channel stiffeners and the radiator compartment cowls by several permanently riveted interlocking stiffeners.

Wing

Wing profile root: NACA 0015, close to wing tips NACA 23009. Angle of the wing setting +20.

The wing center section is in two parts, forward and trailing edges, both of which are designed as integral parts of the forward fuselage and wing outer panels.

The forward structure is built up of six principal parts: a forward and a rear beam corresponding precisely to the main beams in the outer wing panels, two inner bulkheads, and two outer bulkheads for splicing to the outer wing panels.

The two internal bulkheads consist of reinforced aluminium web sections riveted to extruded aluminium forming members. The outboard bulkheads, too, are reinforced webs with extruded angle forming members.

Web sections are heavily reinforced where the wing bolts cut through from the outer panel beams to fittings on the center section beams

Top and bottom skin sections are formed aluminium sheet, reinforced with angle stringers and heavy plate where holes are cut for wing bolt access doors

The wing center section trailing edge consists of a single beam which acts as a carry-through member for the auxiliary beam of the outer wing panels. This beam is built up of formed sheet. Its sections are tied across by a heavy T-section extrusion further reinforced by extruded angle sections. Each side is cut through to accommodate air ducts to the Prestone radiator, which is mounted just aft of these beams and extends up through the longitudinal beams of the forward fuselage. The oil radiators are strapped into a compartment formed by the bulkheads ahead of the auxiliary beam.

Outer wing panels are joined to the inner wing section on each side at approximately 22 in outboard of the P-39's centerline of symmetry.

The three spars of the outer wing panel are called (from L.E. to T.E.) „front beam", „rear beam", and „auxiliary beam". Front and rear beams consist of flanged caps strips of extruded aluminium shapes

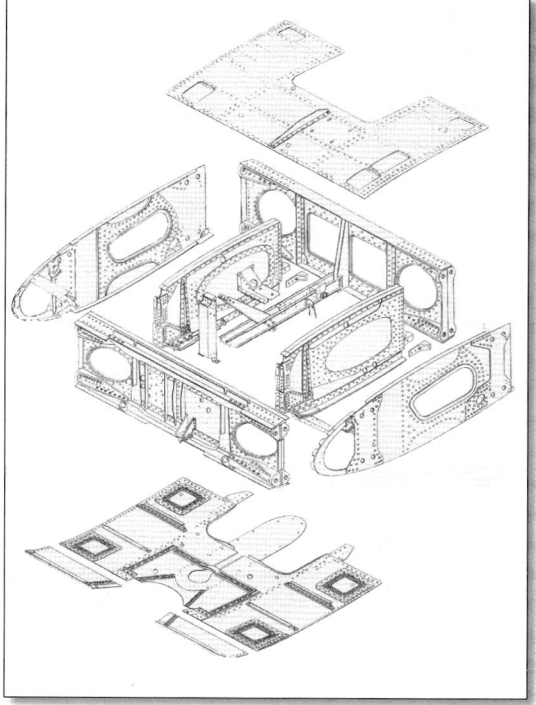

milled to distinctive and exacting dimensions with the flange thickness tapering from a maximum of 0.865 in at the inboard end to 0.154 in at the outer tip. Solid heavy gauge aluminium sheet webs with occasional stringers complete the beam construction.

The auxiliary beam is made up of formed aluminium capstrips with a solid aluminium web.

There are 13 principal wing panel bulkheads of pressed and beaded aluminium, ranging in gauge from .072 for the inboard splice bulkhead to .064 for the wing-tip splice bulkhead.

In the Bell production set-up, the bulkheads are numbered in stations from one to ten. Counting inboard, the first seven bulkheads are whole-numbered stations. The eighth bulkhead is Sta. 7.5, and each represents a half station from there to the thirteenth bulkhead at Sta. 10.

Compartments formed by bulkhead Sta. 2 to Sta. 7.5 between front and rear beams accommodate the self-sealing fuel cells. A longitudinal bulkhead between Stas. 4 and 5, about one-third of the distance forward from the rear to front beam, forms a compartment for the main landing gear retracting spindle assembly. Twin .30-cal machine guns are installed between Stas. 7.5 and 8, with a false rib bulkhead between them.

An intercostal beam of formed, blanked, and beaded aluminium sheet webbing between drawn aluminium capstrips runs between Stas. 8 and 10, about midway between the front and rear beams, forming a compartment with the front beam to accommodate wing ammunition boxes.

The landing gear wheel wells between Stas. 1 and 2 are shaped of formed and drawn aluminium capstrips with formed aluminium sheet webbing. Two angle-shaped stringers extend from Sta. 1 bulkhead over the top of the wheel well to the outer periphery to reinforce the wing catwalk.

Wing Skin

The lower surface wing skin is in three principal sections, forward and aft of the rear beam, and the leading edge. Each section consists of two panels running inboard to approximately Sta. 7.5 and from there to Sta. 10.

The two panels are .025-gauge formed sheet with numerous reinforced access door cutouts. The inboard panel between rear and forward beams is .051-gauge formed sheet, largely built up with reinforcing panels. The outboard front panel is .032-gauge sheet with a large access door of the same gauge aluminium for the wing ammunition cases. The leading edge is .032-gauge formed sheet.

The skin from top to lower surface consists of panels similar in arrangement and gauge. The inboard forward panel has a number of reinforced access holes for fuel tanks; the outboard forward panel has a large door for installation or removal of wing guns. Skin stringers are, for the most part, Z-section, rolled or drawn aluminium. Flush riveting is used.

The wing tip comprises two bulkheads and three tapering beams. The wing splice bulkhead is built up of rolled capstrip and sheet webbing of .064-gauge aluminium. Tip edge is a formed aluminium strip enclosing the skin, which is .032 gauge entirely flush riveted.

Ailerons

Ailerons are fabric covered monospar structures of the „Frise" type with built-up ribs of extruded shapes in some cases and formed ribs in others. Leading edge ribs are formed and blanked sheet riveted to the .040-gauge Alclad beam. Trailing edges are formed strips enclosing the skin fabric.

Trim and Servo Tabs

Controllable trim tabs of laminated phenolic plastic are located at the trailing edge of each inboard aileron. These trim tabs also act as a servo control through a mechanical linkage which automatically rotates the tab to an angle opposite to the movement of the aileron An additional servo tab of laminated plastic, not controllable by the pilot, is located just outboard of the trim tabs.

Wing Flaps

The wing flaps are split trailing edge type and form the lower rear surface of the outer wing panels. They extend from Sta. 1 to the inboard end of the aileron. Attached to the wing by a piano type hinge extending the full flap length, they are connected to the auxiliary beam lower flange. Flaps are operated by a push-pull tube and an electrically driven connecting link mechanism. The operating member consists of five turnbuckle connecting links between the flap beam and the push-pull tube.

The single beam is a formed channel section of .040-gauge aluminium. Ribs are formed solid sheet sections in two parts, riveted fore and aft of the beam. Skin stringers are also formed channel flanged sections. Skin is a solid panel of .025-gauge sheet. A doubler sheet with a number of blanked lightening holes is riveted to the ribs forward of the beam. The flaps are stressed so that full extension (43 deg.) may be used at 150 mph max speed.

The horizontal stabiliser is constructed as a single unit with sections cut away in the center to permit access of the vertical stabiliser to the fuselage. It is a twin-spar structure of conventional stressed skin design. The forward beam is constructed in three flanged sections formed of heavy gauge sheet.

Stabilizer tips are single formed aluminium sections riveted to the single rib of the stabiliser proper. Four threaded studs, two on each beam, provide for attaching the stabiliser to the aft fuselage with lock nuts.

Elevators

Fabric covered elevators are similar in construction to the ailerons. Right and left hand elements are joined at the control quadrant by tubular steel members spliced by forged, flanged steel collars. The left elevator has a trim tab fastened to an auxiliary beam just forward and inboard of the trailing edge section. Two hinge settings are installed on the main beam and attached to the horizontal stabiliser. A mass-balance, tubular-shaped weight, used for dynamic and static balancing, is located in the foremost section of the leading edge.

Vertical Stabilizer

The vertical stabiliser is similar in structure to the horizontal stabiliser, except that beams are one piece construction. A hole is cut in the skin on both sides for the navigation light installation. Cast fittings are installed on the projecting ends of the main and rear beams for attachment by nuts and bolts to the aft fuselage. Two hinge fittings are riveted to the aft flange of the rear beam for the rudder attachment.

The fabric covered rudder is similar in structural arrangement to the elevators and ailerons. The top and bottom portions are covered by formed and beaded aluminium sheet. Two hinge fittings for fastening to the vertical stabiliser and rudder control quadrant are installed on the main beam. The auxiliary beam supports a plastic trim tab, and a round mass-balanced weight is mounted in the fore-most section of the leading edge.

Nine pieces of formed aluminium sheet and formers comprise the empennage fillet assembly, which is attached by flush screws and channel nuts.

Pilot's Cabin

The cabin with its six transparent panels, arranged for maximum visibility, is in two sections: the forward cabin, a built-up structure superimposed upon and forming an integral part of the forward fuselage ahead of the engine; and the removable aft cabin enclosure directly over the engine and joining the forward section at the turnover beam.

The forward section consists of drawn aluminium frames for the glass and Plexiglas enclosures as well as the formed aluminium skin sides forward of the door. Directly ahead of the pilot is a windshield panel of ¼ in laminated shatter proof glass; two side windshield panels are 1/4 in convex Plexiglas and directly overhead is a panel of 5/32 in Plexiglass formed to the cabin contour. All panels are set in rubber channel retainer strips.

Aluminium automobile type doors are located on both sides of the cabin. Both have a 21/64 in roll down laminated glass panels operable on the ground or in the air at any speed in level flight. Emergency door release handles, painted red, are just forward of each door frame in the cockpit. Both cabin doors are held tightly closed by a door latch at the top to prevent the door from opening at high speeds. This fastening is broken when the emergency handle is operated.

The pilot's seat is bucket-type, metal construction, and non-adjustable. A Type B-11 Sutton safety harness is attached to the seat with a roller mechanism and is released or locked by a control under the seat. The cabin is designed to accommodate a pilot 5 ft. 8 in high, weighing 200 lb. with parachute.

The turnover bulkhead behind the pilot is of extremely rigid construction capable of withstanding loads consider-ably in excess of the airplane weight. It consists of two main beams of very heavy gauge aluminium tied together by a number of formed and blanked bulk-head sections and heavy gauge formed aluminium skin, flush riveted to the beams and bulkheads.

The aft cabin is a shallow streamline structure conforming to fuselage contours. It consists of channel formers and a beaded aluminium deckplate for housing a portion of the radio installation. It is enclosed by two convex panels of 5/32 in Plexiglass.

Differing from the forward pilot cabin, which is permanent, the aft cabin section is removable. It joins the forward section at the turnover.

Landing Gear

The Airacobra is equipped with a fully retractable tricycle landing gear. Nose wheel is self-castoring, non-steer-able type and retracts up and aft into the forward fuselage; the main wheels retract up and inboard into the outer wing panels. Retracting mechanism is operated by an electric motor through a system of torque tubes, universal joints, gear boxes, and splined connections. In the event of power failure, the wheels can be operated by an emergency ratchet crank at the right of the pilot's seat.

Cleveland Pneumatic Tool air-oil shook struts are used on both nose and main gear.

The main wheels are magnesium alloy equipped with 10.0 Hx5 disk type hydraulic brakes. Main wheel tire casings are 26x6 in, 6-ply, rayon, with high pressure, puncture proof tubes. Three types of interchangeable tires are used.

Retracting Mechanism

The landing gear is operated by a reversible, 24-volt motor giving 3/4 hp. at 3,800 rpm. Incorporated in the assembly are a clutch and reduction gear drive with a 40 to 1 ratio.

Nose wheel retraction mechanism consists of a retracting screw installed in the forward fuselage and driven by the landing gear motor through torque tubes and a 90-deg. gear drive.

The emergency handcrank is equipped with a ratchet and can be reversed by a switch at the top outboard face of the crank. A clutch handle is located just aft and outboard of the handcrank on the cabin floor, to change from electric to manual operation or vice versa.

Landing Gear Fairings

The main wheel fairing is made up of three sections. Two are attached to the main wheel strut at two points. The third section of fairing, known as the „flipper door," is hinged to the lower surface of the wing center section. Upon retraction, the tire comes in contact with the spring loaded-arm causing it to fold upward, drawing up the door.

The nose wheel fairing is in two sections. One is bolted to the top of the nose wheel strut and lies flush with the undersurface of the fuselage when the wheel is retracted. The other section consists of right and left-hand doors hinged to the forward fuselage at four hinge points. These doors are actuated by a spring loaded arm in a manner similar to the main wheel fairing doors.

Engine and Accessories

The Allison Type Y1710 engine is mounted on four „Fabreeka" pads inserted between the engine mounting points and airplane beam fittings. It is secured by eight bolts and nuts arranged in four pairs, through fittings riveted to the inboard side web beneath the top longitudinal beam flange. A propeller reduction gearbox is located in the fuselage nose and is bolted to the forward bulkhead. The gear boss is connected to the engine by a 10-ft drive shaft operating at crankcase speed. This shaft runs through the beam fuselage under the pilot's seat and consists of a flanged coupling and center bearing. The reduction gear hose has a separate oil system.

The exhaust system is comprised of dual stacks, six on each side, of formed seam-welded stainless steel with sand blast finish. Stacks are welded to mounting flanges for attachment to the engine.

Fuel System

The fuel system consists of two 60 gal. tanks integrally built into the outer wing panels. The left wing tank includes a reserve area of 20 gal. A droppable auxiliary fuel tank of either 75 or 150-gal capacity may be carried in the bomb rack suspended from the wing center section.

Fuel is supplied to the carburettor by a pressure pump, located on the rear of the engine accessory housing, augmented by either two

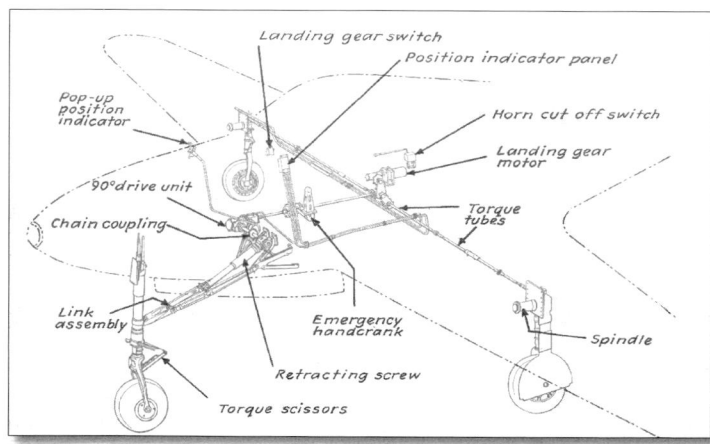

booster fuel pumps in the wing, or by a single booster pump in the wing center section Booster pumps are electrically driven and are used for starting, warm weather takeoff and high altitude flying to prevent vapour lock.

A primer pump is installed at the lower right-hand side of the radio control panel. It is hand-operated and draws fuel from the booster pump and injects it into the engine intake manifold system.

Fuel Tanks

Each fuel tank consists of six leak-proof fuel bags. The left wing tank is equipped with two finger-type fuel strainers, one providing for normal fuel consumption, and the other for reserve fuel consumption. The right-hand tank includes only one finger strainer providing for consumption of the entire tank content.

Oil System

Engine lubricating oil is circulated by the main pressure pump having a built-in check valve, and a scavenger pump located at the lower right-hand side of the engine accessory housing. Oil is supplied to the pressure pump "In" from the bottom of the tank and circulates through the engine. Oil leaves the engine from the main scavenger pump "Out" and is delivered equally to each of the oil coolers and returns through parallel lines connecting to a single line attached to the top of the oil tank. The propeller reduction gearbox is lubricated by a separate oil circulating system with its own tank and pump.

The engine main oil tank, of 13.8-gal capacity, is constructed of seam welded magnesium alloy sheet located in the aft fuselage behind the engine accessory bay on the airplane centerline.

Oil Cooling System

The oil cooling system consists of two oil coolers with separate air ducts located within each outer wing panel and connecting to each cooler in the wing center section. The coolers incorporate an independent, fully automatic, thermostatically controlled by-pass valve which circulates oil along the cooler coil until the oil is properly cooled.

Cooling System

Engine is cooled by a high-temperature, liquid Prestone cooling system. The Prestone radiator is of the cartridge core type, constructed in two sections and assembled as a single unit in a radiator mounting cradle. The assembly is mounted on four flexible vibration insulating units below the engine, between the longitudinal beams aft of the wing carry through rear beam. Coolant is carried in lines from the outlet on the top forward end of each cylinder head to the radiator. Coolant enters the radiator through a compound inlet on each side of the radiator top and flows downward and rearward re-turning to the coolant circulating pump inlet collector.

Electrical System

The electrical system is of the single conductor type, shielded and protected by rigid and flexible conduits. A main electrical control switch panel is rigidly mounted to a metal box for shielding and is located to the left of the cockpit main instrument panel,

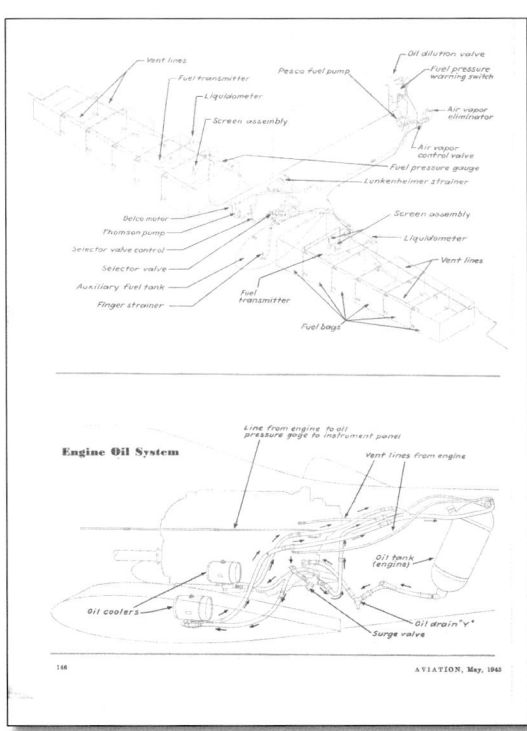

A standard a.e. type battery is mounted in the forward fuselage between the .50-cal. fuselage guns and beneath the gun compartment cowling, aft of the reduction gear box.

Engine Starting System
Electrically operated, inertia type engine starters are used on the P-39 mounted near the bottom right hand side of the engine accessory housing. A starter pedal is located on the right hand side of the cockpit floor.

Generator and Booster Coil
An engine-driven generator is mounted on the engine accessory housing to the rear. The generator control panel is mounted on vibration absorbing units and is installed in a structural enclosure within the left side of the fuselage. A generator relay is operated by toggle switch on the main electrical control panel.

Landing Light
A three-focus electric retractable landing light assembly is installed flush with the lower surface of the left-hand outer wing panel. It can be lowered and stopped at any intermediate position or retracted by means of an electric motor controlled from a switch on the main control panel.

Heating and Ventilating System
The cabin is heated by two 3 in metal tubes which take hot air from directly behind the Prestone radiator, and expel it to two ducts on the cabin floor between the pilot's seat. Cool air is supplied to the cabin by two ducts which take air from the Prestone cooling duct just forward of the radiator. Cool air is emitted to the cabin through the same ducts as the hot air. Selection of hot and cold or mixed air is controlled by two butterfly flaps, one of which is located on each duct.

Vacuum System
A vacuum pump is mounted on the rear of the engine and is used for forming a vacuum essential for operation of certain instruments. Pump includes a suction line from the instrument panel and an exhaust line to the Peseo oil separator. A relief valve is mounted on top of the vacuum pump to prevent over exertion of suction on the instruments.

De-icing Equipment
De-icing equipment includes a glycol spray to prevent formation of ice on the windshield and a propeller blade de-icing installation. Both units are supplied from a single glycol tank mounted in the gun compartment of the forward fuselage.

P-39D-1, serial 41-38401 of Maj. Norman "Coach" G. Morris, CO of 35th FS, 8th FG, Milne Bay. 1942. (Darryl Ford)

Engine maintenance. (US National Archive)

Above: *P-39N-5-BE, serial 42-18802, details of the nose. See also photo at page 37.*
Below: *P-39L during engine maintenance. (Both US National Archive)*

Bell P-39 Airacobra

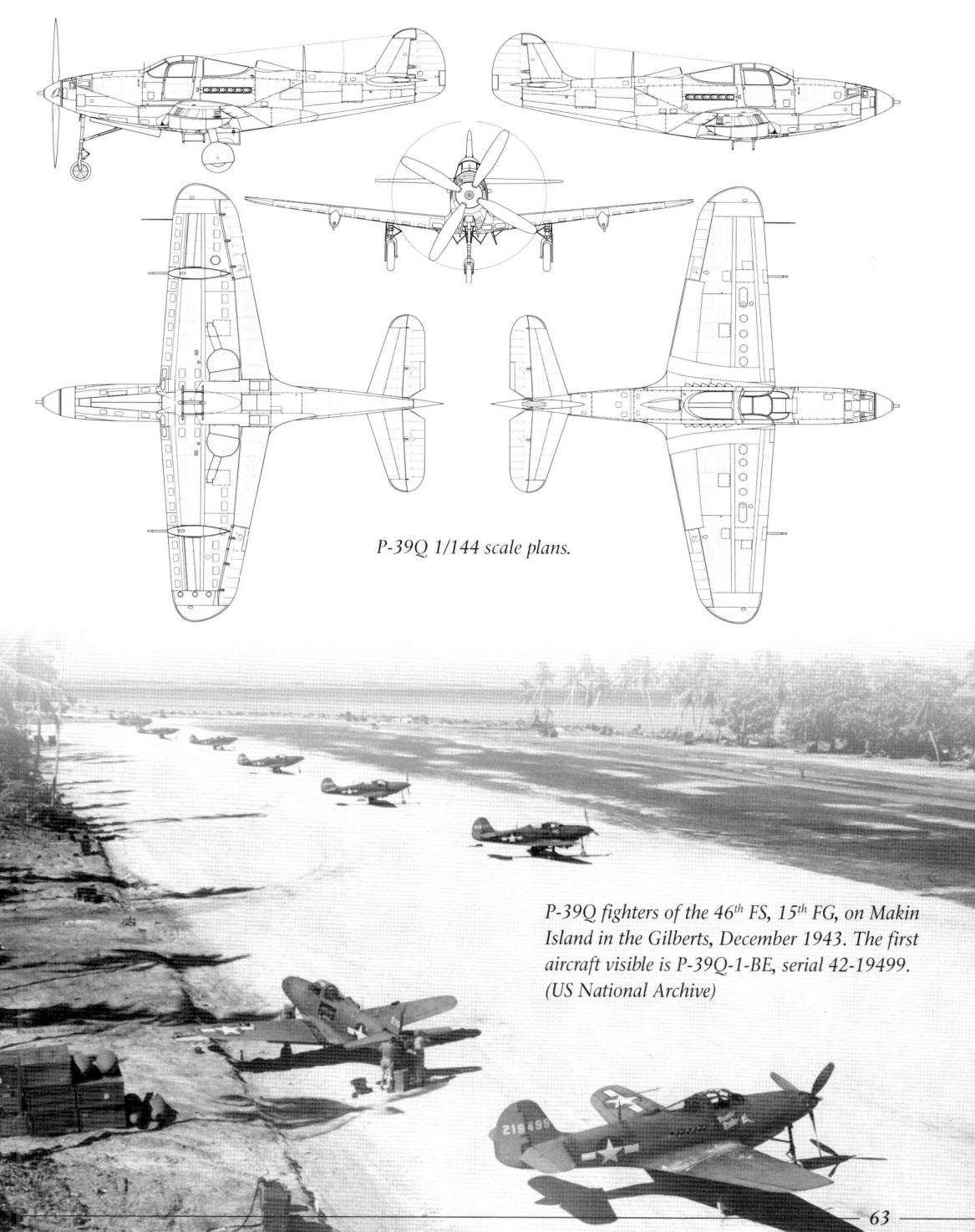

P-39Q 1/144 scale plans.

P-39Q fighters of the 46th FS, 15th FG, on Makin Island in the Gilberts, December 1943. The first aircraft visible is P-39Q-1-BE, serial 42-19499. (US National Archive)

List of Soviet P-39 Aces

Name Original in Cyrillic In transcription	Hero of Soviet Union	UNIT	Ind. victories	Shared victories	Sorties/combats	Remarks	Aircraft
Покрышкин Александр Иванович Pokryshkin Aleksandr Ivanovich	***	16 GIAP	59	6	650/156		P-39D-2 (41-38520) "white 13" P-39N-0 (42-9004) "white 100"
Гулаев Николай Дмитриевич Gulaev Nikolay Dmitrievich	**	129 GIAP	57	3	248/69	on P-39 32 vict.	
Речкалов Григорий Андреевич Rechkalov Grigoriy Andreevich	**	16 GIAP	56	6	450/122		P-39D-2 (41-38547) "white 40" P-39N-0 (42-8747) P-39Q-15 (44-2547) "white PGA"
Глинка Дмитрий Борисович Glinka Dmitriy Borisovich	**	100 GIAP	50		300/90		P-39K-1 (42-4403) "white 21"
Алелюхин Алексей Васильевич Alelyukhin Aleksey Vasil'evich	**	9 GIAP	40	17	601/258	on P-39 26/11	
Лавриненков Владимир Дмитриевич Lavrinenkov Vladimir Dmitrievich	**	9 GIAP	36	11	48/134		
Камозин Павел Михайлович Kamozin Pavel Mikhaylovich	**	68, 101 GIAP	35	13	200/70	on P-39 23/6	
Смирнов Алексей Семенович Smirnov Aleksey Semenovich	**	28 GIAP	34	1	457/?		
Бабак Иван Ильич Babak Ivan Il'ich	*	100 GIAP	33	4	330/103	POW 22.04.1945	P-39D-2 (41-38416) P-39N-0 (42-9033) "white 01"
Комельков Михаил Сергеевич Komel'kov Mikhail Sergeevich	*	104 GIAP	32	7	321/75		
Клубов Александр Федорович Klubov Aleksandr Fedorovich	**	16 GIAP	31	19	457/95	KIA 1.11.44	P-39N-1 (42-9434) "white 45" P-39N-1 (42-9689) "white 125"
Головачев Павел Яковлевич Golovachev Pavel Yakovlevich	**	9 GIAP	31	1	457/125		
Бобров Владимир Иванович Bobrov Vladimir Ivanovich	*	129, 104 GIAP	30	20	451/112	13/4 in Spain	
Амет-хан Султан Amet-khan Sultan	**	9 GIAP	30	19	603/150	on P-39 6/8	
Архипенко Федор Федорович Arkhipenko Fedor Fedorovich	*	129 IAP	30	14	467/102	on P-39 26/4	
Карасев Александр Никитович Karasev Aleksandr Nikitovich	*	9 GIAP	30	11	380/112	POW 7.04.44	
Лихобабин Иван Дмитриевич Likhobabin Ivan Dmitrievich	*	72 GIAP	30	9	321/60		
Глинка Дмитрий Борисович Glinka Dmitriy Borisovich	*	100 GIAP	30		200/?		P-39D-2 (41-38431)
Новичков Степан Матвеевич Novichkov Stepan Matveevich	*	67 GIAP	29		315/?		
Кожевников Анатолий Леонидович Kozhevnikov Anatoliy Leonidovich	*	212 GIAP	27		300/69		
Ковачевич Аркадий Федорович Kovachevich Arkadiy Fedorovich	*	9 GIAP	26	6	520/?	on P-39 13	
Сиротин Вячеслав Федорович Sirotin Vyacheslav Fedorovich	*	17 IAP	26		300/?		
Борисов Иван Григорьевич Borisov Ivan Grigor'evich	*	9 GIAP	25	8	250/86		
Балюк Иван Федорович Balyuk Ivan Fedorovich	*	54 GIAP	25	5	500/135	on P-39 8/2	
Шикунов В. Д. Shikunov V. D.		9 GIAP	25		?		
Егоров Алексей Александрович Egorov Aleksey Aleksandrovich	*	212 GIAP	24	7	271/66		
Лавицкий Николай Ефимович Lavitskiy Nikolay Efimovich	*	100 GIAP	24	2	250/100	KIA 10.03.44	
Чепинога Павел Иосифович Chepinoga Pavel Iosifovich	*	213 GIAP	24	1	100/?		
Труд Андрей Иванович Trud Andrey Ivanovich	*	16 GIAP	24	1	600/71		

Bell P-39 In Detail

Fuselage

Above: Reconnaissance version - P-39N-3-BE serial 42-8838 in Italy 1944 of unknown unit. Original wartime colour photo. (T. Kopański coll.)

Below: P-39Q in Soviet markings. Aircraft preserved in Finnish Museum Keski-Suomen Ilmailumuseo in Tikkakoski. (M. Orlog)

Airacobra during overhaul. (US National Archive)

Bell P-39 In Detail

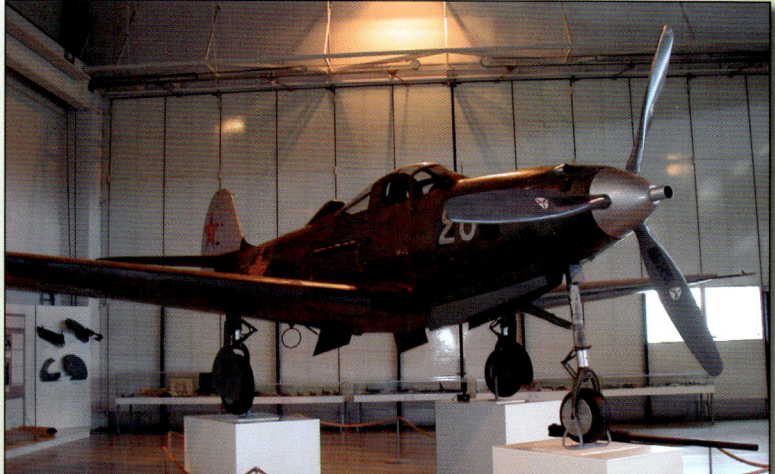

Three photos of P-39Q in Finnish museum. Aircraft still in original camouflage (not repainted in museum, after the war). Note that Soviet P-39Q were not fitted with underwing guns. (All photos M. Orlog)

Bell P-39 In Detail

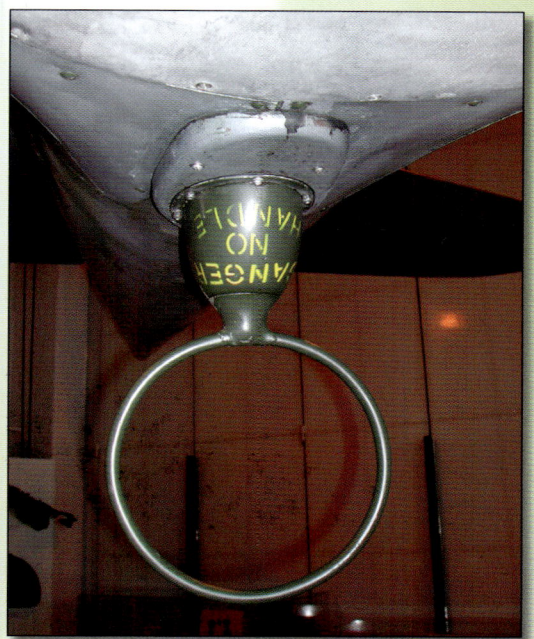

Opposite page top: Nose of the P-39Q.
Opposite page middle:
P-39Q middle fuselage from the right. Note how USAAF markings was repainted in Russia.
Opposite page bottom:
Fuselage of P-39K in one of the USA museums.
(All photos M. Orlog)

Above and right: Details of the direction-finder loop mounted on Soviet Airacobras.
Below: Photo of the right, middle part of the fuselage.
(All photos M. Orlog)

69

Right: Aerial mounting at the top of the fuselage.

Below: Details of the engine covers and air intake, from the right.

Bottom of the page: Two photos of the forward, starboard part of the fuselage.
(All photos M. Orlog)

Bell P-39 In Detail

Nose of the P-39Q from the right. (M. Orlog)

P-39N, bottom, center between main gear. Prestone radiator, oil cooling-shutters on either side, coolant shutter in center. (A. Lochte)

Rear fuselage, port side of P-39N. Aircraft during restoration with panels removed and not painted yet. (A. Lochte)

Bell P-39 In Detail

Above:
Port fuselage of P-39N during restoration. Engine not fitted.

Right:
P-39N, port side, rear of the engine compartment.

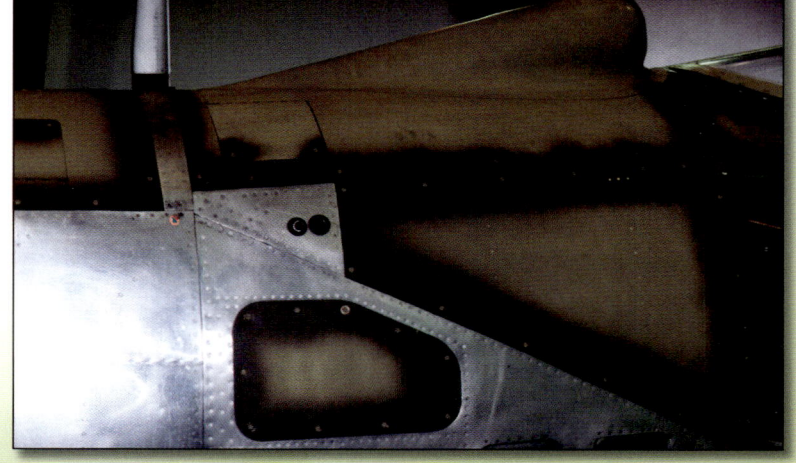

P-39N. Carburettor air intake, starboard side. Note that removeable panels are painted.
(All photos A. Lochte)

Bell P-39 In Detail

P-39N. Coolant shutter in open position, bottom, looking forward.

P-39N. Gun compartment, starboard side, looking forward. Yellow tank is for oxygen. All guns are removed.

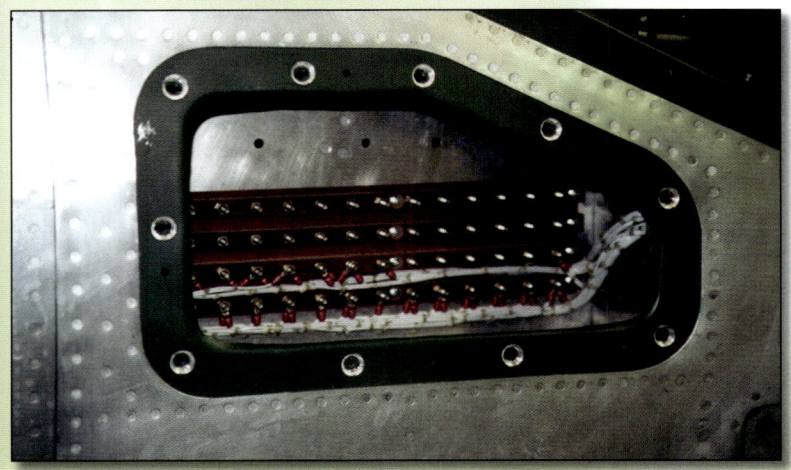

P-39N. Rear fuselage, starboard side. Access to electrical connections

(All photos A. Lochte)

73

Bell P-39 In Detail

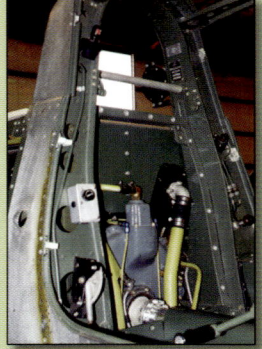

Above:
P-39N. Starboard, rear of the cockpit, looking aft, with seat removed.

Right:
P-39N. Port side of the cockpit. Engine and seat removed, looking forward.

P-39N.
Port side, bottom of the nose.

(All photos A. Lochte)

Bell P-39 In Detail

Right:
Port side of the nose of P-39N.

Below:
Front view of P-39N spinner with Aeroproducts propeller.

(All photos A. Lochte)

Below:
Starboard side of the P-39N fuselage.

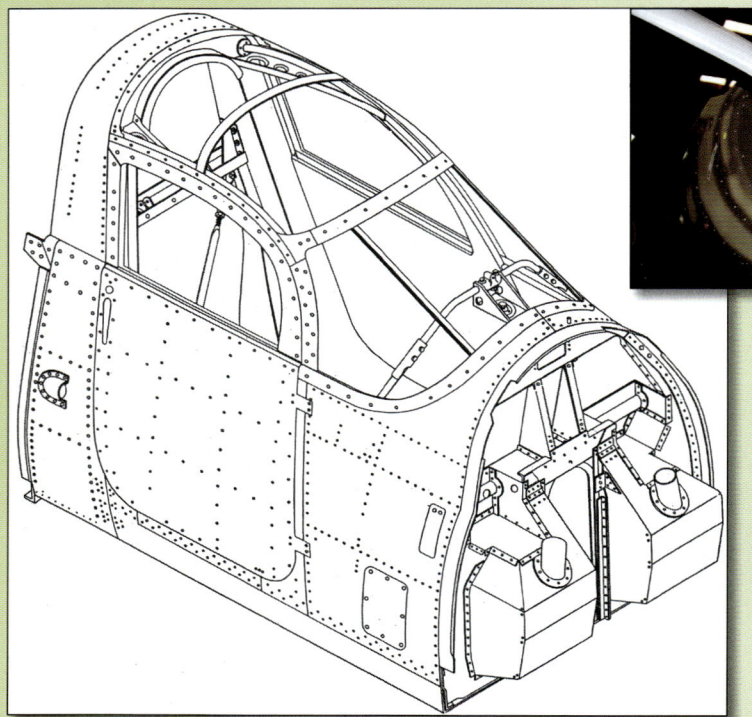

Above:
P-39N spinner.

Left:
Cockpit compartment. Drawing from Technical Manual

Below:
Port side of P-39N. fuselage.
(Photos A. Lochte)

Bell P-39   In Detail

Two photos of the port side of P-39N during restoration.
Nose in the upper photo and rear part of the fuselage in the lower one.

Below:
P-39N engine compartment, port side, looking to the rear. Engine oil tank (silver) is visible
(All photos A. Lochte)

P-39Q, bottom of the nose, port side.
(A. Lochte)

P-39Q, rear, port side of the fuselage. First Aid access panel is visible.
(A. Lochte)

Below:
P-400 fuselage stations and skin thicknesses. Drawing from Structural Repair Manual.

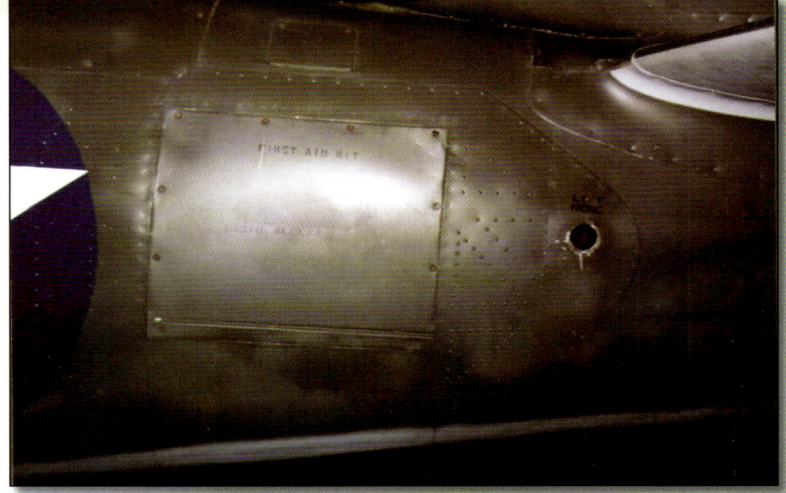

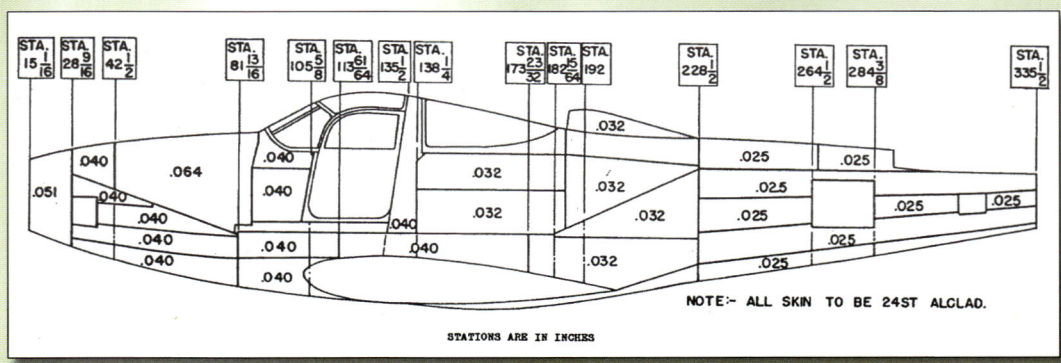

Bell P-39 In Detail

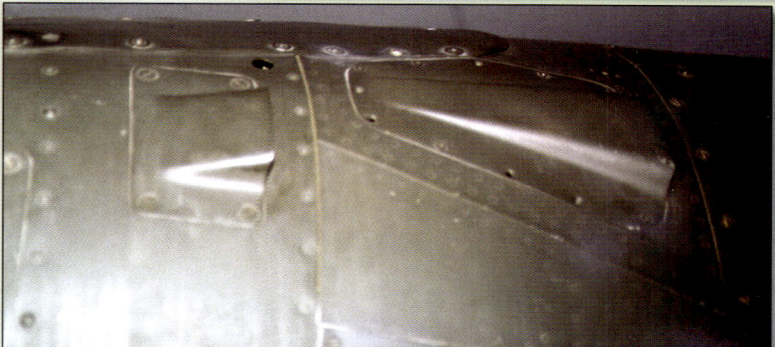

Left:
P-39N, starboard side of the nose. Gun cooling vents are visible. Please note the panel lines and riveting.

Middle:
Gun cooling vents, in focus, on the port side of P-39Q.

Bottom left:
P-39N, starboard side. One outlet is expansion tank vent.

Bottom right:
P-39N, starboard side of the nose. Gun outlet and gun cooling vents are visible.

(All photos A. Lochte)

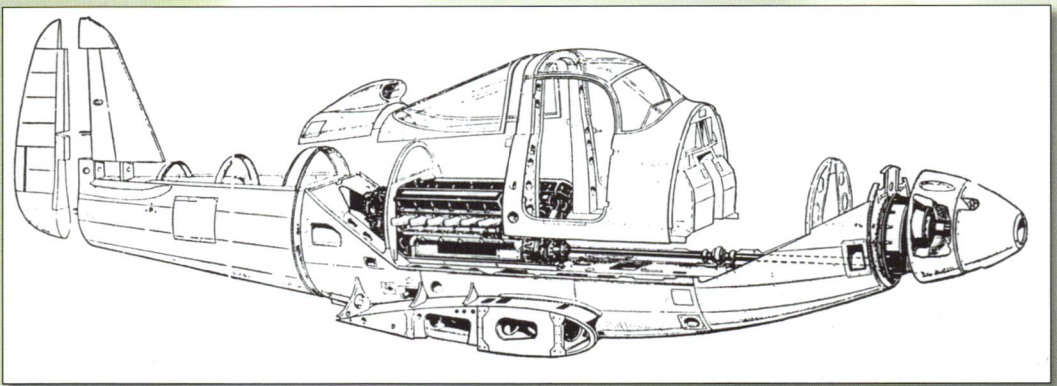

Top:
Starboard side of the P-39N nose. (A. Lochte)

Above:
Fuselage structure as shown in Technical Manual.

Left:
P-39N, underside of the port side nose. (A. Lochte)

CANOPY

Above: Canopy of the P-39 "Racker-II" at Hawaii. Note the gun sight in front of the cockpit, which is missing on the most preserved aircraft. (US National Archive)
Below: Starboard side of the cockpit canopy, P-39N. (A. Lochte)

Above:
Aft canopy and air intake.

Right:
Forward part of the canopy, starboard side.

Below:
Windscreen of P-39N, 3/8 inch armour plate in front of windscreen.
All photos of P-39N.
(Photos A. Lochte)

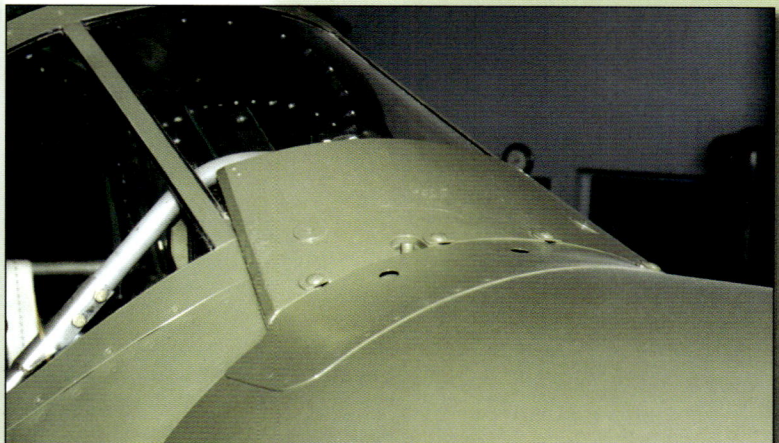

P-39N, windscreen armour plate.

P-39N, port side of the front canopy.
Photos (A. Lochte)

P-39Q, starboard side of the windscreen. (M. Orlog)

COCKPIT

Opposite page:
Cockpit photo of a preserved P-39. (A. Lochte)

Left: P-39D lower front panel.

1. Tachometer.
2. Parking Brake Handle.
3. Clock.
4. Fuel Pressure Gauge
5. Temperature Gauge (Atmospheric).
6. Suction Gauge.
7. Manifold Pressure Gauge.
8. Oil Temperature and Pressure Gauge.
9. Fuel Quantity Gauge (Dual Reading).
10. Carburettor Temperature Gauge
11. Oil Pressure Gauge (Reduction Gear Box).
12. Temperature Gauge (Prestone).
13. Ignition Switch (Magneto and Battery).
14. Valve (Static Pressure Selector).
15. Left Hand Charging Handle (.50 Calibre Gun).
16. Right Hand Charging Handle (.50 Calibre Gun).
17. Brake Pedal.
18. Valve (Vacuum Source Selector).
19. Tuning Control (Radio).
20. Rudder Bar.
21. Transmitter Control (Radio).
22. Volume Control (Automatic or Manual, Radio Receiver).
23. Charging Handle (37-mm Cannon).
24. Volume Control (Manual, Radio Receiver).
25. Shell Ejection Dumping Control (37-mm Cannon).
26. Hi-Lo Control (Radio Receiver).
27. Control (Bomb Release).
28. Primer Pump Control (Engine).
29. Arming Lever.
30. Loading Handle (37-mm Cannon).
31. Switch Box (Radio Receiver).
32. Crank Mounting (Landing Gear Manual Operation).

P-39D left side of the cockpit.
57 Toggle Switch (Instrument Lights)
58 Control Knob (Manual Operation Propeller Pitch)
59 Control Knob (Carburettor Mixture)
60 Control Handle (Window Operating)
61 Control Knob (Throttle)
62 Push Button (37 mm Cannon Operation)
63 Indicator, Flaps (Mechanical)
64 Handle (Door Operating)
65 Toggle Switch (Flap Control)
66 Toggle Switch (Landing Gear Control)
67 Handles, Gun Charging (30 Cal Wing Guns)
68 Door Catch (Auxiliary)
69 Toggle Switch (30 Cal. Wing Guns)
70 Toggle Switch (50 Cal. Fuselage Guns)
71 Toggle Switch (37 mm Cannon)
72 Control Knob (Rheostat, Gun Sight)
73 Toggle Switch (Camera Gun)
74 Safety Switch (Propeller)
75 Ammeter (Generator)
76 Toggle Switch (Cabin Heater)
77 Toggle Switch (Cabin Lights)
78 Toggle Switch (Oil Dilution Valve)
79 Toggle Switch (Running Lights)
80 Toggle Switch (Landing Light)
81 Control Knob (Rheostat, Directional Instrument)
82 Control Stick
83 Auxiliary Switch Box
W Toggle Switch (Auto. Or Manual Control Propeller)
85 Toggle Switch (Generator Control)
86 Toggle Switch (Pitot Heater)
87 Indicators (Landing Gear, Mechanical)
88 Trigger Control (30 & 50 Cal Guns)
99 Main Switch Box

P-39D right side of the cockpit.

14. Valve (Static Pressure Selector)
18. Valve (Vacuum Source Selector)
36. Armour Glass
39. Cockpit Light
60. Control Handle (Window Operating)
64. Handle (Door Operating)
67. Handles, Gun Charging (30 Cal. Wing Guns)
68. Door Catch (Auxiliary)
90. Instrument Light (Flourescent)
91. Fuel Warning Signal
92. Control Damper (Cockpit & Gun Heater)
93. Toggle Switch (Fuel Warning Signal)
94. Chart (Frequency In Kilocycles, Radio)
95. Handle (Emergency Door Release)
96. Oxygen Gauge (Cylinder Pressure & Flow)
97. Starter Pedal (Electric)
98. Control Valve Knob (Oxygen Flow)
100. Warning Signal Light (Cabin Heater)
101. Adjustment Lever (Rudder Bar)
102. Eye Bolt (Parking Harness)

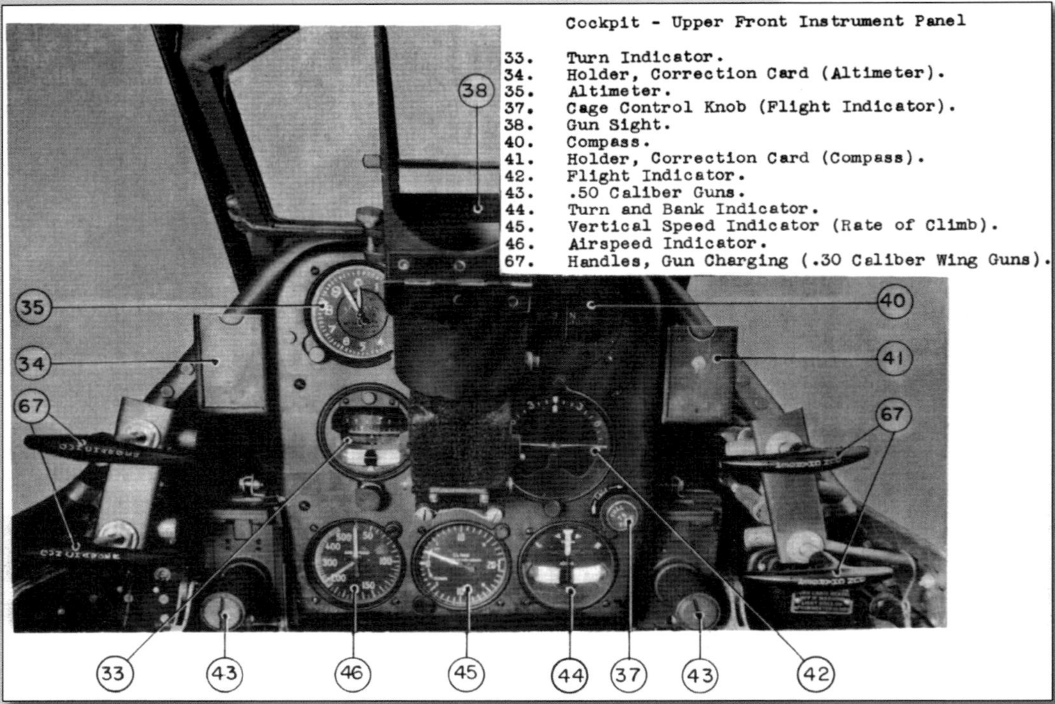

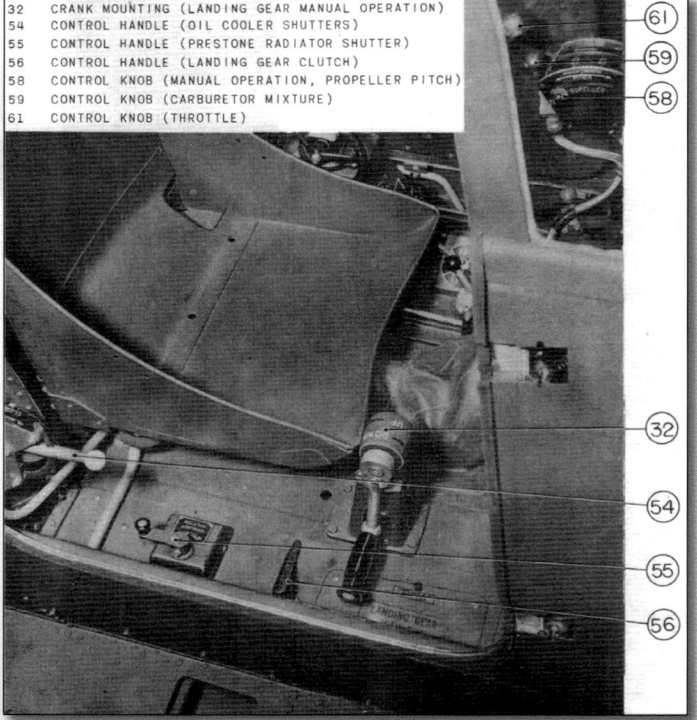

Cockpit - Upper Front Instrument Panel
33. Turn Indicator.
34. Holder, Correction Card (Altimeter).
35. Altimeter.
37. Cage Control Knob (Flight Indicator).
38. Gun Sight.
40. Compass.
41. Holder, Correction Card (Compass).
42. Flight Indicator.
43. .50 Caliber Guns.
44. Turn and Bank Indicator.
45. Vertical Speed Indicator (Rate of Climb).
46. Airspeed Indicator.
67. Handles, Gun Charging (.30 Caliber Wing Guns).
38
35
40
34
41
67
67
33
43
46
45
44
37
43
42

Above: *P-49D. Upper Front Instrument Panel.*

Right: *P-39 D. Right side of the floor.*

32 CRANK MOUNTING (LANDING GEAR MANUAL OPERATION)
54 CONTROL HANDLE (OIL COOLER SHUTTERS)
55 CONTROL HANDLE (PRESTONE RADIATOR SHUTTER)
56 CONTROL HANDLE (LANDING GEAR CLUTCH)
58 CONTROL KNOB (MANUAL OPERATION, PROPELLER PITCH)
59 CONTROL KNOB (CARBURETOR MIXTURE)
61 CONTROL KNOB (THROTTLE)
61
59
58
32
54
55
56

29	ARMING LEVER
47	COCKPIT LIGHT
48	CONTROL (CARBURETOR HEAT)
49	CUTOUT SWITCH (LANDING GEAR WARNING SIGNAL)
50	CONTROL KNOB (RUDDER TRIM TAB)
51	CONTROL WHEEL (ELEVATOR TRIM TAB)
52	CONTROL KNOB (AILERON TRIM TAB)
53	SELECTOR VALVE (FUEL)
89	CONTROL LEVER (WOBBLE PUMP)

P-39D. Left side of the floor.

P-39D front armoured glass. Photo from the Technical Manual.

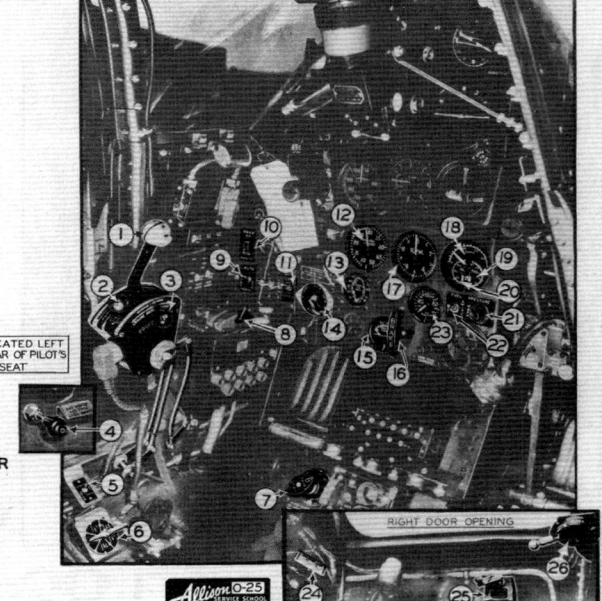

Opposite page:
P-39K. Front view of the cockpit.

1. Altimeter
2. Gun Sight
3. Compass
4. Flight Indicator
5. Turn And Bank Indicator
6. Climb Indicator
7. Turn Indicator
8. Air-Speed Indicator
9. Tachometer
10. Manifold Pressure Gauge
11. Engine Cage Unit
12. Prestone Thermometer
13. Carburettor Thermometer
14. Liquidometer
15. Clock
16. Oil Pressure Gauge
17. Suction Gauge
18. Radio Clock
19. Parking Brake
20. 50 Calibre Gun Charger
21. Gun, Cannon And Gun Camera Switches
22. Gun Sight Rheostat
23. Battery Switch
24. Flap Switch
25. Ammeter
26. Navigation Light Switches
27. Pitot Heater Switch
28. Fuel Booster Pump Switch
29. Propeller Control Switch
30. Ignition Switch
31. Generator Control Switch
32. Landing Lamp Rheostat
33. Engine Control Quadrant
34. Cannon Stick Switch
35. Control Switch
36. Harness Adjustment
37. .30 Calibre Wing Gun Chargers
38. Bomb Arm & Safe Lever
39. Bomb Release
40. 37 Mm Shell Loader Handle
41. 37 Mm Shell Charger Handle
42. Receiver Control Box
43. Engine Primer Pump
44. Radio Control Panel
45. Starter Foot Switch
46. Rudder And Brake Pedal
47. Heater Switch
4«. Rudder Pedal Adjustment
49. Radio Relay Switch Box

50. Emergency Door Release Handle
51. Fuel Pressure Warning Signal Light
52. Turn And Bank Throttle Valve
53. Oxygen Regulator And Cage
54. Glycol Spray Pump
55. Propeller De-Icer Rheostat
56. Radio Control Box
57. Light Switch Box
58. Fluorescent Cockpit Light
59. Door Latch
60. .50 Calibre Gun
61. Throttle Friction Lock
62. Throttle
63. Oil Dilution Switch

Two photos of P-39M cockpit. Photos from the Technical Manual.

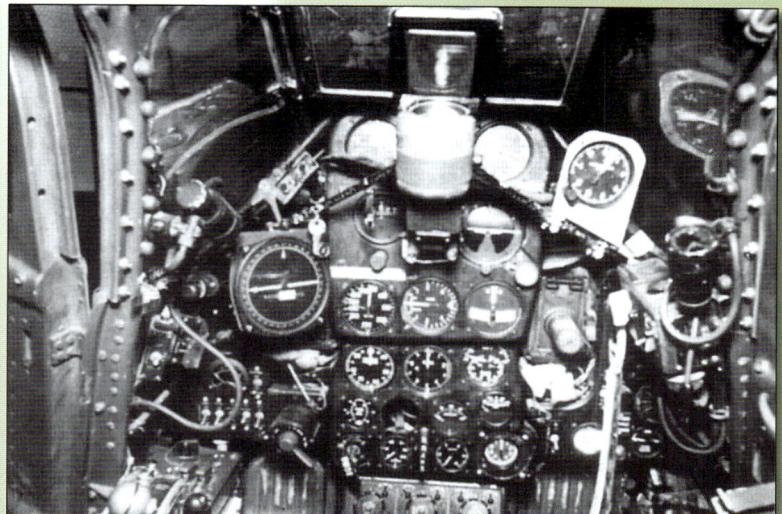

P-39N instrument panel. Photo from the Technical Manual.

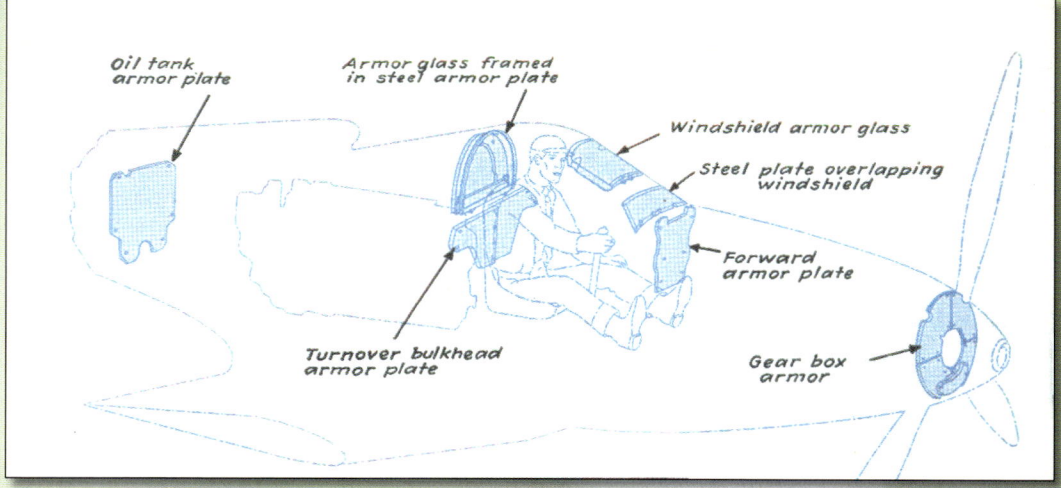

P-39D armour protection.

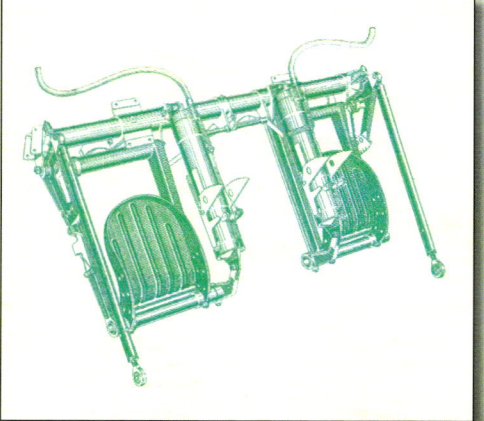

Rudder pedal.
Drawings published in Aeroplane, May 1943.

Cockpit arrangement and pilot's seat harness.

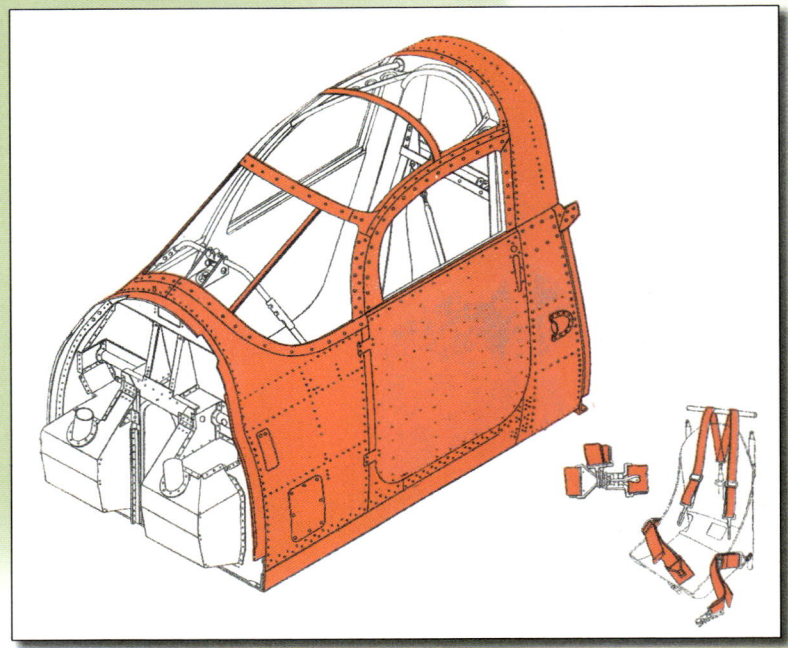

Pilot's seat. Drawings from the Technical Manual.

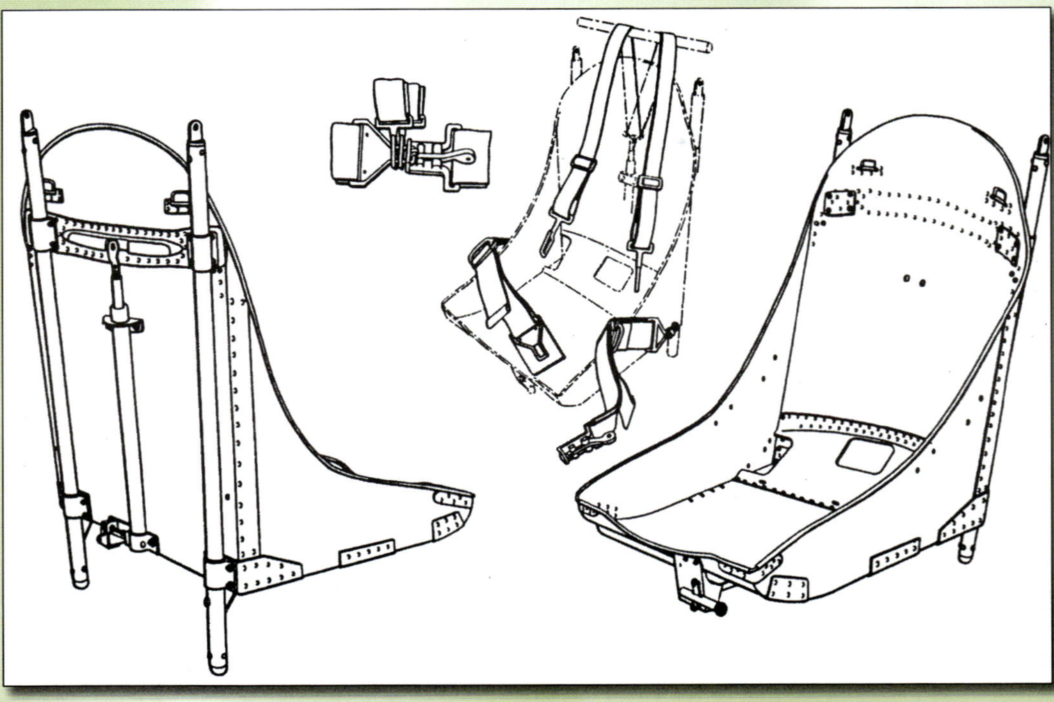

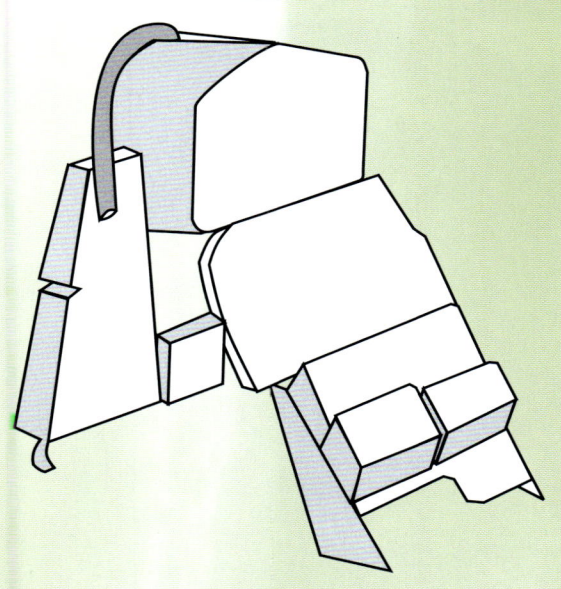
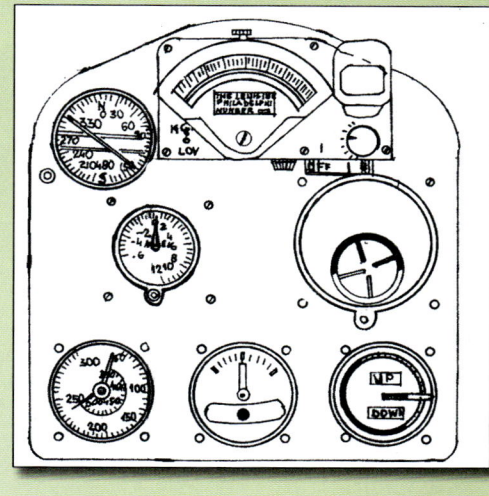
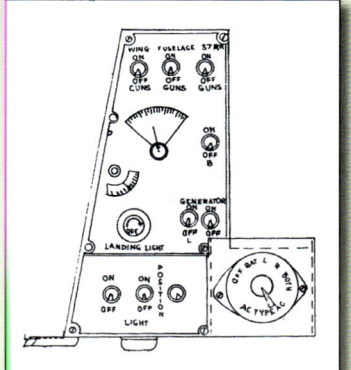
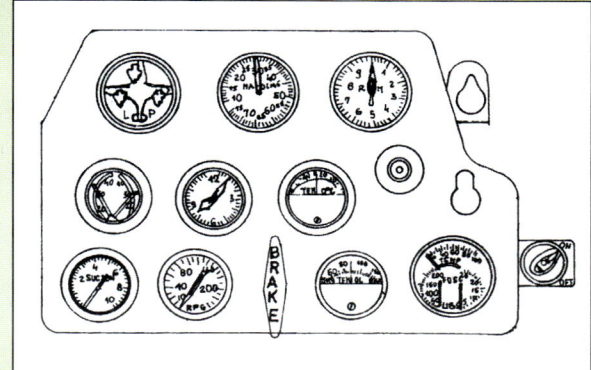

Details of the instrument panels of P-39Q.

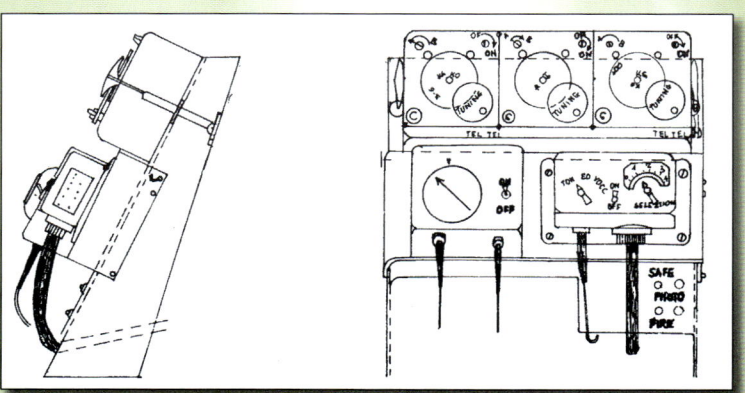

Bell P-39 In Detail

Right: P-39N instrument panel. Just above control column the .50-caliber machine gun is visible. The red gun charging handle is also visible.

Bottom of the page: The handle in the right corner is the landing gear emergency control crank. On the left is oil shutter control and the silver handle in the black housing on the floor is the coolant shutter control.

Opposite page:
Top, left: P-39N instrument panel with N-3 gunsight on the top. In front of the gunsight is the rubber crash pad to protect the pilot.

Top right: Port side door. Open crank (red) is visible and handle to raise and lowered the window (also red, but the lower one).

Bottom left: Details of the left part of the instrument panel and centre console.

Bottom right: Inside of the starboard door, very similar to port one. Data and map case is also visible with fixed instructions how to operate landing gear and flaps.

(All photos A. Lochte)

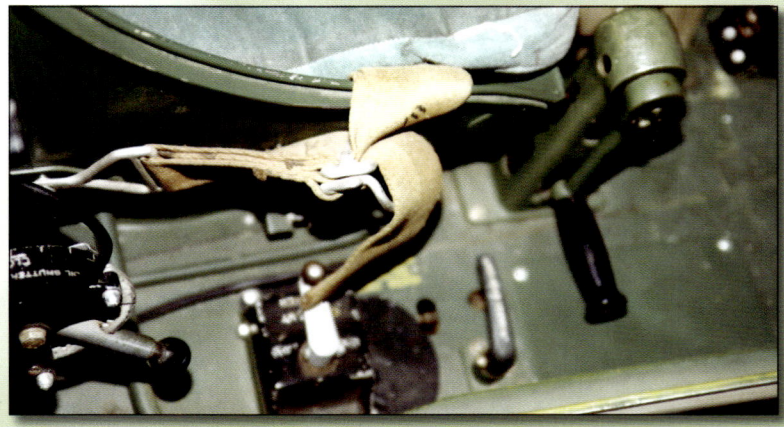

Bell P-39 In Detail

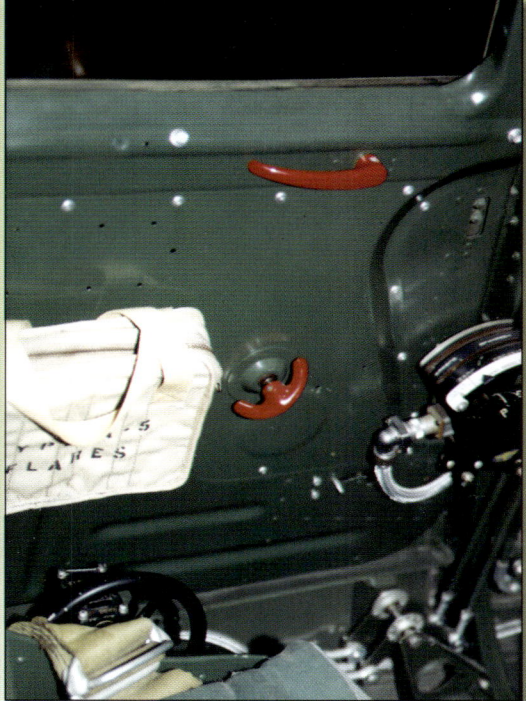

Right:
Details of the N-3 gunsight.

Right, below:
Throttle quadrant mounted on the portside door jamb.

Bottom right:
Drawing showing details of the throttle quadrant.

Bottom left:
Central panel and control column mounting.

(All photos A. Lochte)

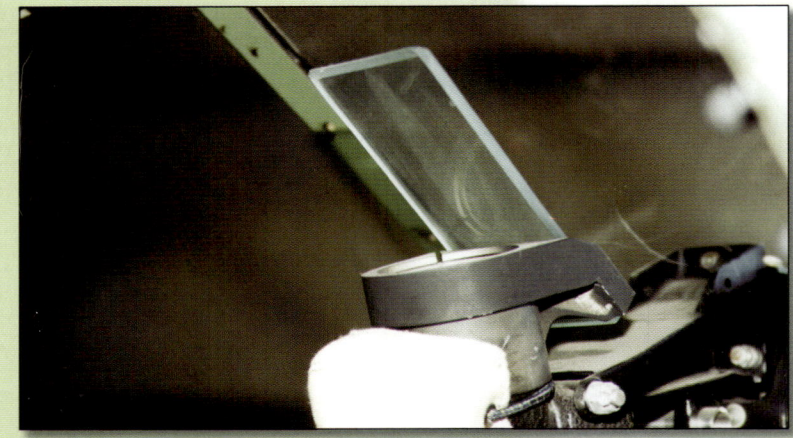

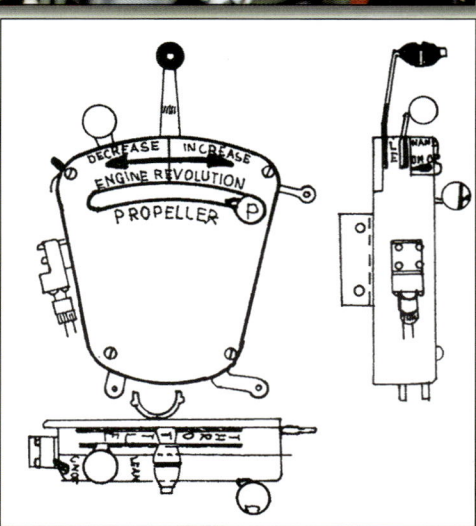

Bell P-39   In Detail

Above:
Cockpit from the left, door removed. Note how the throttle quadrant (1) is mounted.

To the right:
Photos of the P-39N cockpit details.
(All photos A. Lochte)

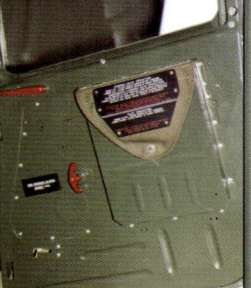

WING

Two photos of P-39 undersurfaces. Note the early WWII markings - "US ARMY".
This is a P-39Q altered to represent an earlier Airacobra variant. For example, mockups of the wing guns are visible. (A. Lochte)

Bell P-39 In Detail

Top: Preserved ammunition box cover of the P-39Q-21 serial 44-3401. Aircraft crashed in Poland in 1944. Note preserved original wartime colours. (via B. Belcarz)

Middle: P-39Q, starboard wing with aileron visible.

Left: P-39Q, Starboard wing - middle part. (Photos M. Orlog)

Bell P-39 In Detail

Prestone radiator with coolant shutter closed. Oil shutter on the left, also in closed position. P-39Q.

Series of three photos showing glycol cooler intake (inboard) and oil cooler intake (outboard). P-39Q. (All photos M. Orlog)

P-39N, bottom of center fuselage and wing. Aircraft during restoration with cooler intakes removed.

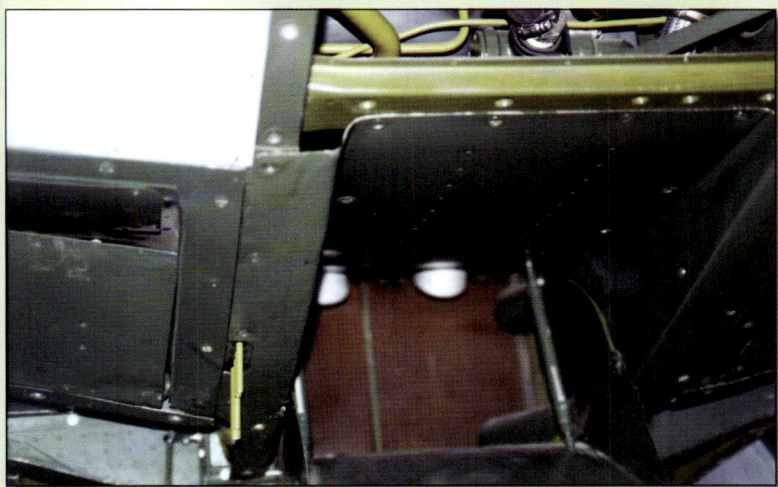

P-39N, bottom looking forward. Prestone radiator with coolant shutter open and oil shutter in closed position (to the left).

P-39N, bottom of the starboard wing, not painted yet.

(All photos A. Lochte)

P-39N. Bottom of the starboard wing tip. Navigation and formations lights are visible.

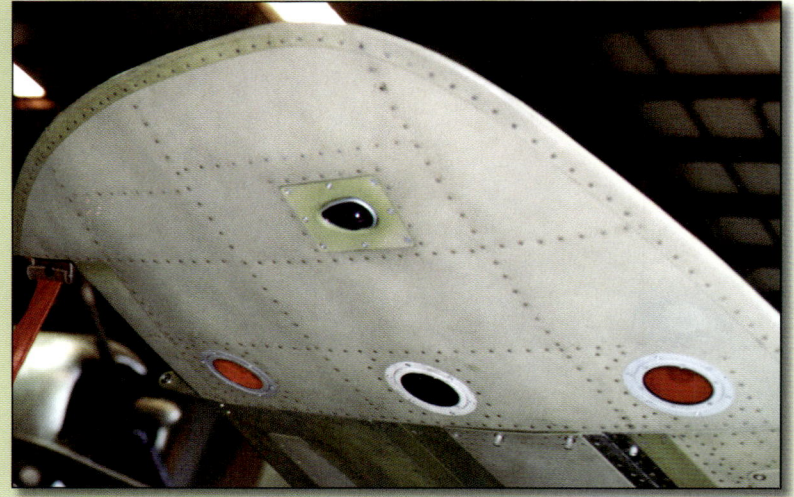

P-39N, bomb rack under the port wing.

Bottom of the port wing. Aircraft during restoration.
(All photos A. Lochte)

Bell P-39 In Detail

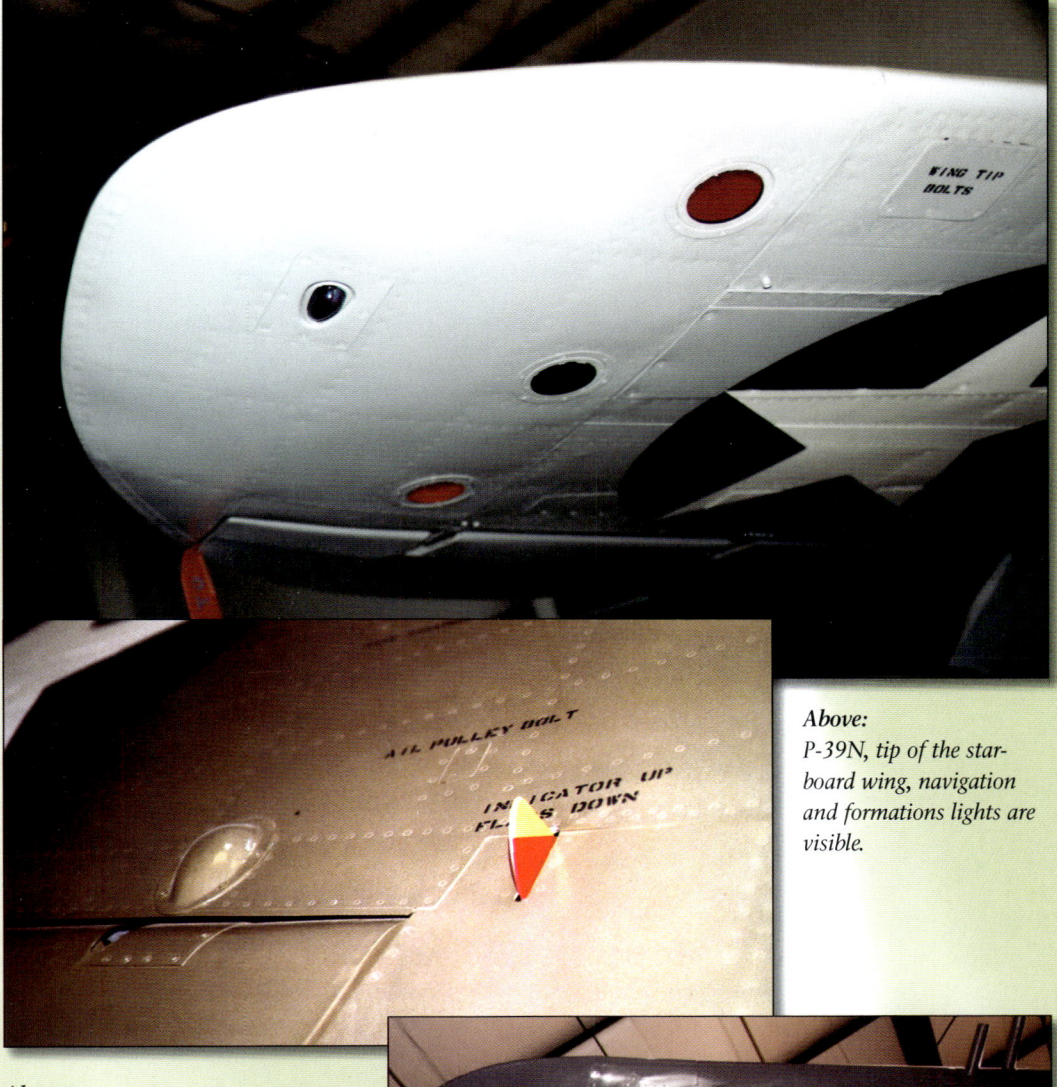

Above:
P-39N, tip of the starboard wing, navigation and formations lights are visible.

Above:
P-39N, flap indicator on the port wing.

Right:
P-39Q, starboard wing tip, bottom view.

(All photos A. Lochte)

P-39N, top of the port wing.

P-39N, top view of the ailerons, inboard.

P-39Q, glycol and oil cooler intakes- port side.

(All photos A. Lochte)

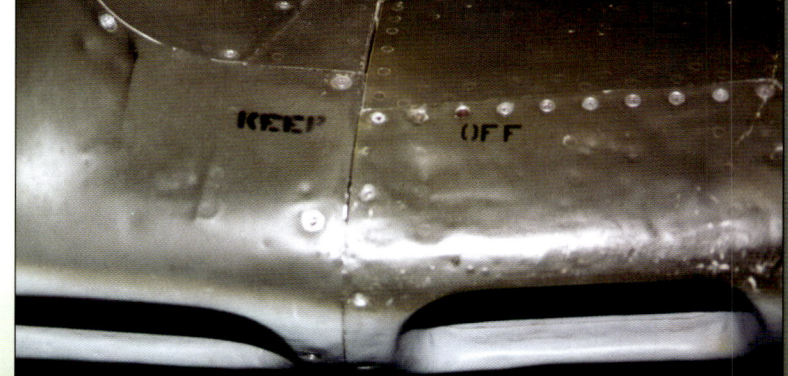

Bell P-39 In Detail

Left: *P-39N, blister cover over aileron linkage, starboard wing.*

Below: *Port landing flap details.*

*Inner end of the starboard landing flap.
(A. Lochte photos)*

107

Engine

Above: Rear view of Allison V-1710 engine.
Below: Port side of Allison V-1710 engine. (Photos A. Lochte)

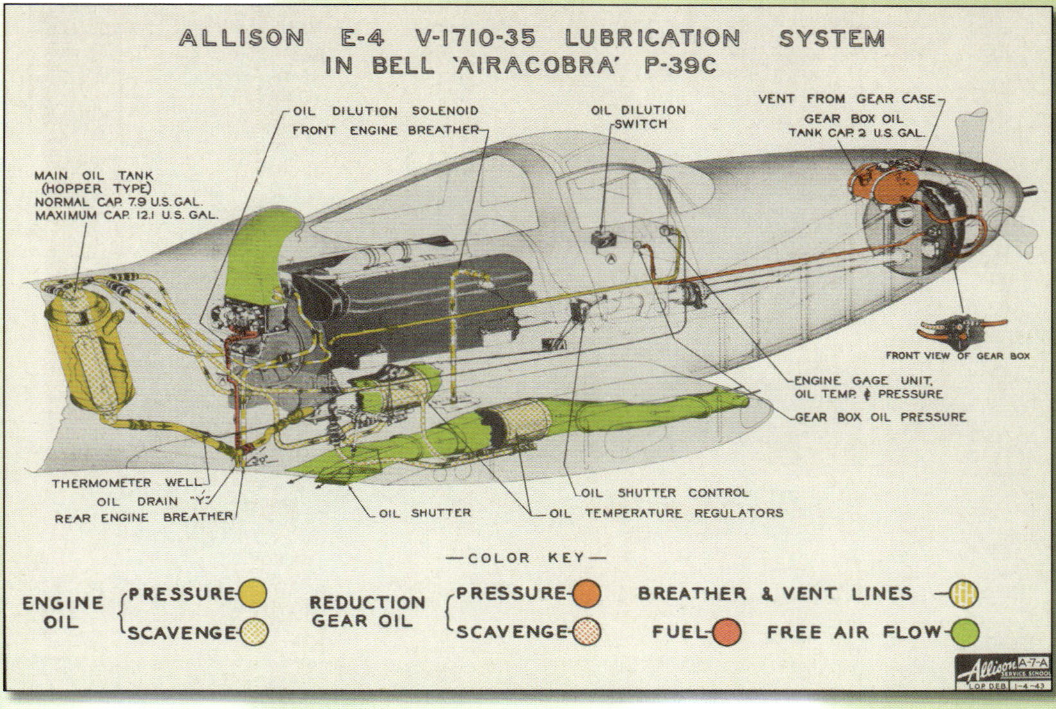

Drawings from the Allison E-4 V-1710-35 Engine Manual.

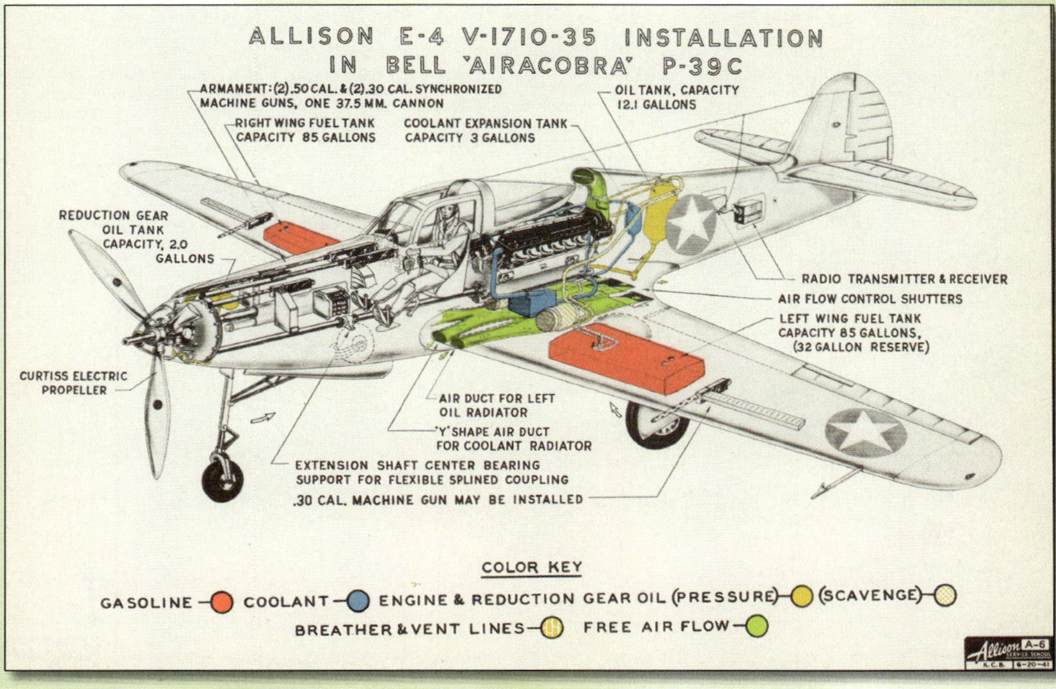

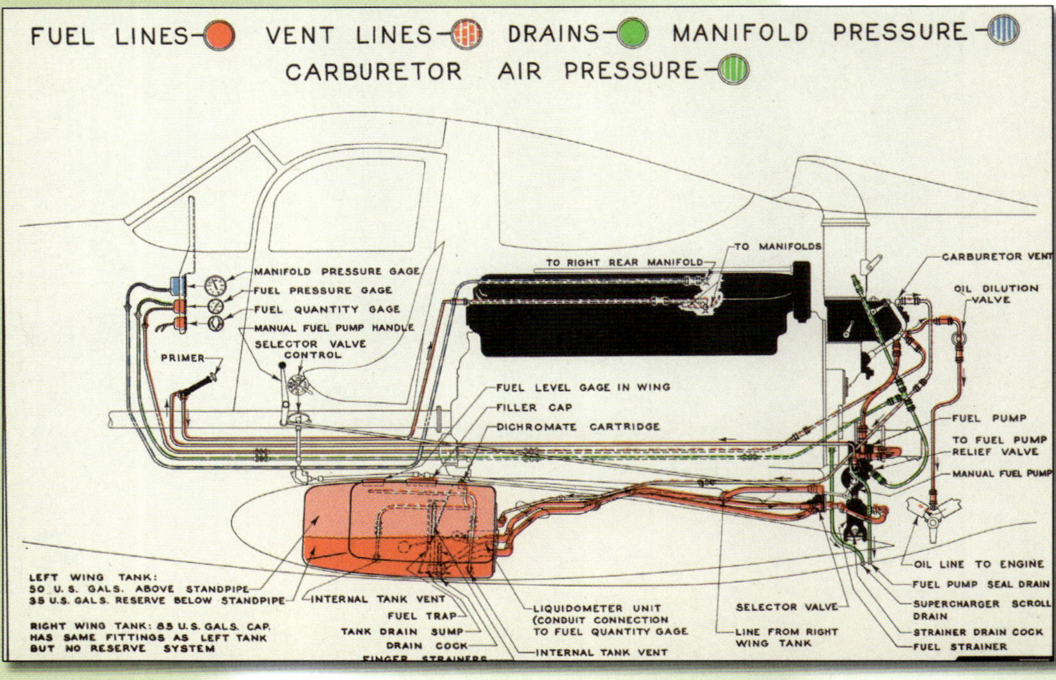

Bell P-39 In Detail

FUEL LINES — **VENT LINES** — **DRAINS** — **MANIFOLD PRESSURE** — **CARBURETOR AIR PRESSURE** —

Labels on upper diagram:
- MANIFOLD PRESSURE GAGE
- FUEL PRESSURE GAGE
- FUEL QUANTITY GAGE
- MANUAL FUEL PUMP HANDLE
- SELECTOR VALVE CONTROL
- PRIMER
- TO RIGHT REAR MANIFOLD
- TO MANIFOLDS
- CARBURETOR VENT
- OIL DILUTION VALVE
- FUEL LEVEL GAGE IN WING
- FILLER CAP
- DICHROMATE CARTRIDGE
- FUEL PUMP
- TO FUEL PUMP RELIEF VALVE
- MANUAL FUEL PUMP
- LEFT WING TANK: 50 U.S. GALS. ABOVE STANDPIPE, 35 U.S. GALS. RESERVE BELOW STANDPIPE
- RIGHT WING TANK: 85 U.S. GALS. CAP. HAS SAME FITTINGS AS LEFT TANK BUT NO RESERVE SYSTEM
- INTERNAL TANK VENT
- FUEL TRAP
- TANK DRAIN SUMP
- DRAIN COCK
- FINGER STRAINERS
- LIQUIDOMETER UNIT (CONDUIT CONNECTION TO FUEL QUANTITY GAGE)
- INTERNAL TANK VENT
- SELECTOR VALVE
- LINE FROM RIGHT WING TANK
- OIL LINE TO ENGINE
- FUEL PUMP SEAL DRAIN
- SUPERCHARGER SCROLL DRAIN
- STRAINER DRAIN COCK
- FUEL STRAINER

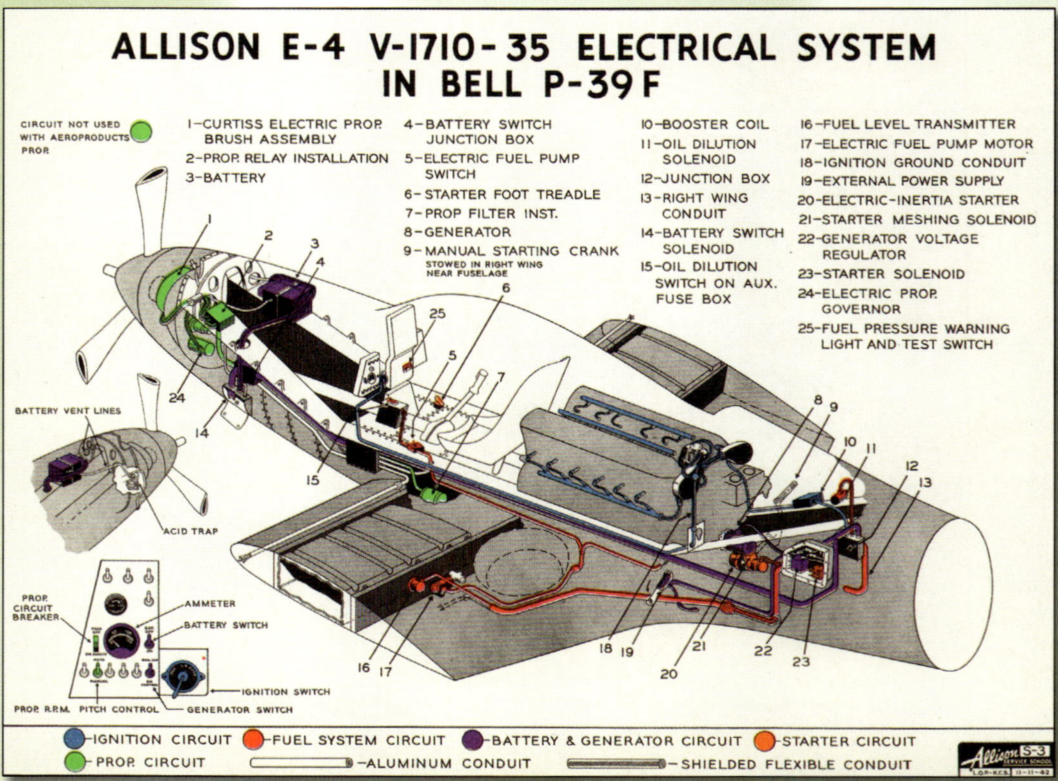

ALLISON E-4 V-1710-35 ELECTRICAL SYSTEM IN BELL P-39F

CIRCUIT NOT USED WITH AEROPRODUCTS PROP.

1 – CURTISS ELECTRIC PROP. BRUSH ASSEMBLY
2 – PROP. RELAY INSTALLATION
3 – BATTERY
4 – BATTERY SWITCH JUNCTION BOX
5 – ELECTRIC FUEL PUMP SWITCH
6 – STARTER FOOT TREADLE
7 – PROP FILTER INST.
8 – GENERATOR
9 – MANUAL STARTING CRANK STOWED IN RIGHT WING NEAR FUSELAGE
10 – BOOSTER COIL
11 – OIL DILUTION SOLENOID
12 – JUNCTION BOX
13 – RIGHT WING CONDUIT
14 – BATTERY SWITCH SOLENOID
15 – OIL DILUTION SWITCH ON AUX. FUSE BOX
16 – FUEL LEVEL TRANSMITTER
17 – ELECTRIC FUEL PUMP MOTOR
18 – IGNITION GROUND CONDUIT
19 – EXTERNAL POWER SUPPLY
20 – ELECTRIC-INERTIA STARTER
21 – STARTER MESHING SOLENOID
22 – GENERATOR VOLTAGE REGULATOR
23 – STARTER SOLENOID
24 – ELECTRIC PROP. GOVERNOR
25 – FUEL PRESSURE WARNING LIGHT AND TEST SWITCH

Additional labels: BATTERY VENT LINES, ACID TRAP, PROP. CIRCUIT BREAKER, AMMETER, BATTERY SWITCH, PROP. R.P.M. PITCH CONTROL, IGNITION SWITCH, GENERATOR SWITCH

Legend:
- IGNITION CIRCUIT
- FUEL SYSTEM CIRCUIT
- BATTERY & GENERATOR CIRCUIT
- STARTER CIRCUIT
- PROP. CIRCUIT
- ALUMINUM CONDUIT
- SHIELDED FLEXIBLE CONDUIT

Allison S-3 — L.GP-R.C.S. 11-11-42

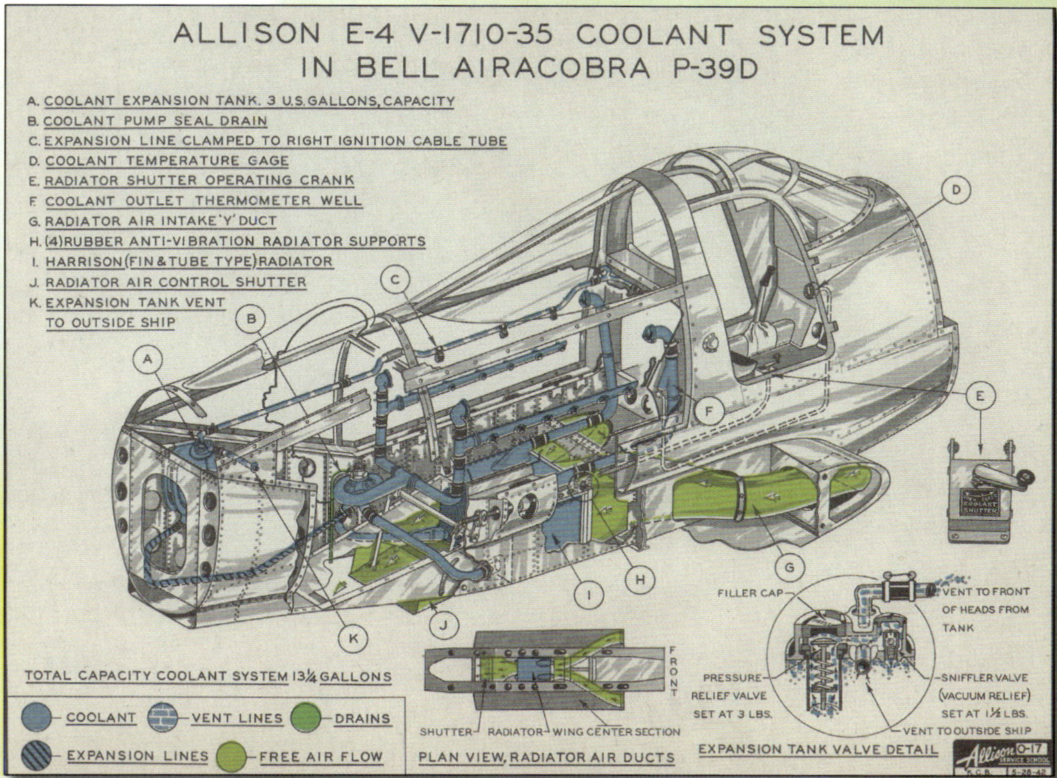

Above and opposite page:
Drawings from the Allison E-4 V-1710-35 Engine Manual.

Right: Engine cross-section.

Preserved Allison V-1710 engine. (Wojciech Łuczak)

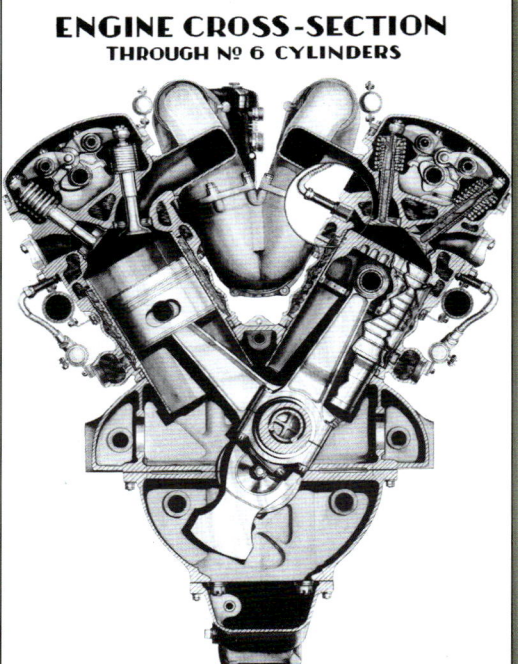

Bell P-39 In Detail

Rear of reduction gear box with extension shaft. Extension center bearing at the right.

P-39N, panel removed, showing the starboard side of the V-1710 engine.

The same engine, but all panels removed. (All photos A. Lochte)

Bell P-39 In Detail

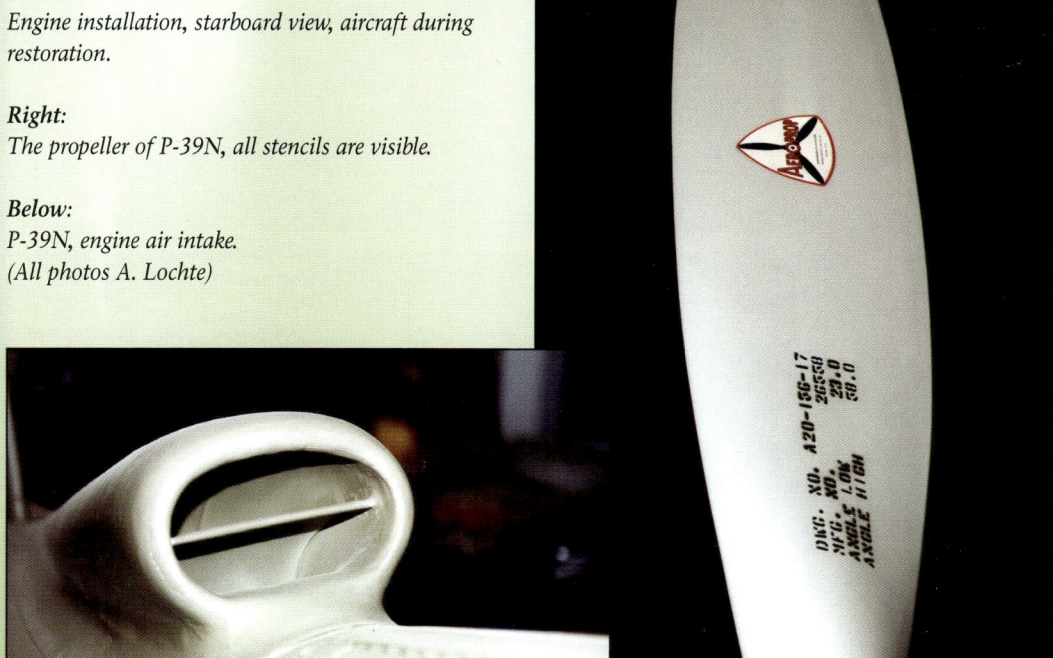

Above:
Engine installation, starboard view, aircraft during restoration.

Right:
The propeller of P-39N, all stencils are visible.

Below:
P-39N, engine air intake.
(All photos A. Lochte)

113

Bell P-39 In Detail

P-39N, portside engine exhaust. (B. Belcarz)

P-39N, starboard engine exhaust. (A. Lochte)

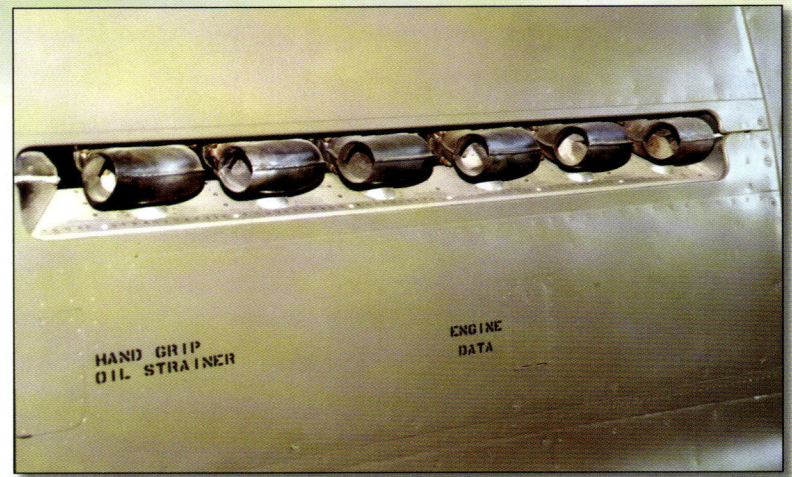

Starboard exhaust of P-39Q. (M. Olrog)

Bell P-39 In Detail

Tail

Above: P-39N, starboard tail profile. (A. Lochte)
Below: P-39Q, lower part of the tail. (M. Orlog)

Bell P-39 In Detail

Above and right:
Two photos of P-39Q rudder and fin. Note the trim tab and rudder hinge.

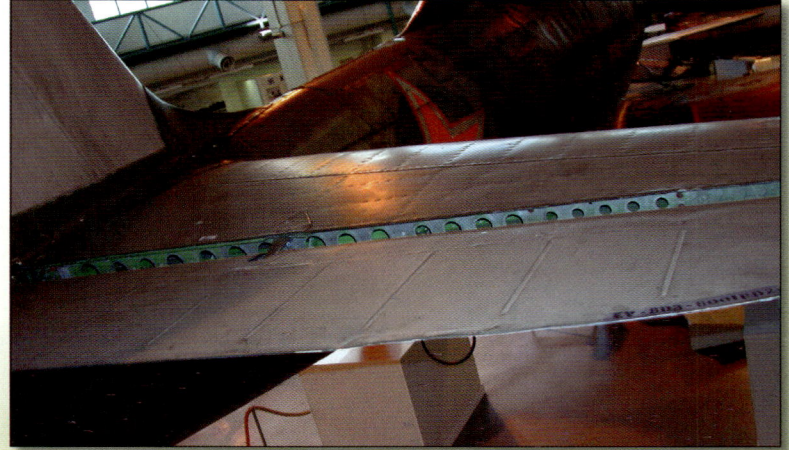

Horizontal tailplane of the same aircraft. (Photos M. Orlog)

Bell P-39 In Detail

Two more photos of the P-39Q fin. In the left photo horizontal stabiliser's fairing is clearly visible.
(M. Orlog (left) and A. Lochte (top) photos)

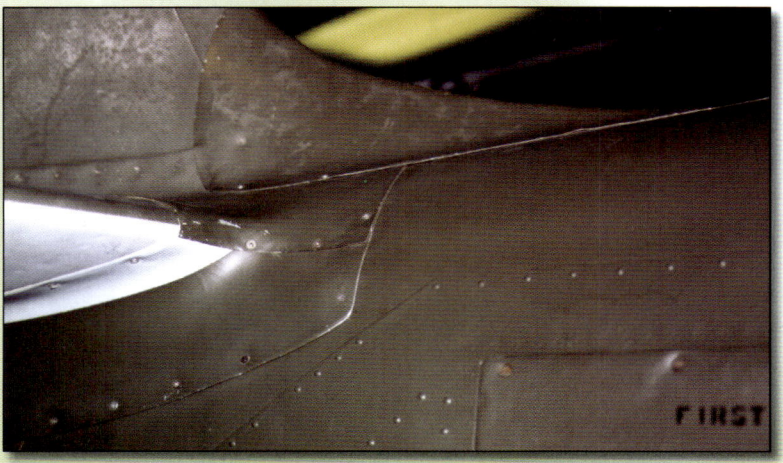

P-39Q, starboard tail fillet. (A. Lochte)

117

Two photos of the horizontal tail surfaces- bottom. (A. Lochte)

Bell P-39 In Detail

Undercarriage

General arrangement of the P-39Q undercarriage. (M. Orlog)

P-39N, inside of the port main gear. (A. Lochte)

119

Bell P-39 In Detail

Above, left: front view of the main leg, looking aft.   *Above, right*: Inside of the portside main undercarriage gear. Note details of the wheel hub disk of the P-39Q, different that of the P-39N shown in the photo on the page 93.
(Photos R. Wallsgrove)

Left: Main leg oleo details. Note the brake pipe.
Below: Main undercarriage inner door.
(Photos A. Lochte)

Bell P-39 In Detail

Above and left:
Two photos of main undercarriage wheel well. (A. Lochte)

Details of the main undercarriage starboard leg. Note how the upper and lower gear doors overlapped. (A. Lochte)

121

Above:
Details of the main undercarriage wheel well, also the oil cooler is visible (yellow) P-39N.

Left and below:
Three photos of the main undercarriage gear of P-39N. Note details of the main leg and how thick is the main gear door.
(Photos A. Lochte)

Starboard main undercarriage leg. (Wojciech Łuczak)

Main undercarriage wheel, inner side. (A. Lochte)

Above: P-39N, Inside of the port main gear wheel well looking outward.

Above: P-39N, starboard, main gear wheel well, looking almost straight up.

P-39Q, outside of the starboard main gear, almost plan view.

All photos (A. Lochte)

Right:
P-39N nose gear from the right.

Below:
Nose undercarriage gear, starboard side.

Below, right:
Nose gear, the retraction arm details.

(All photos A. Lochte)

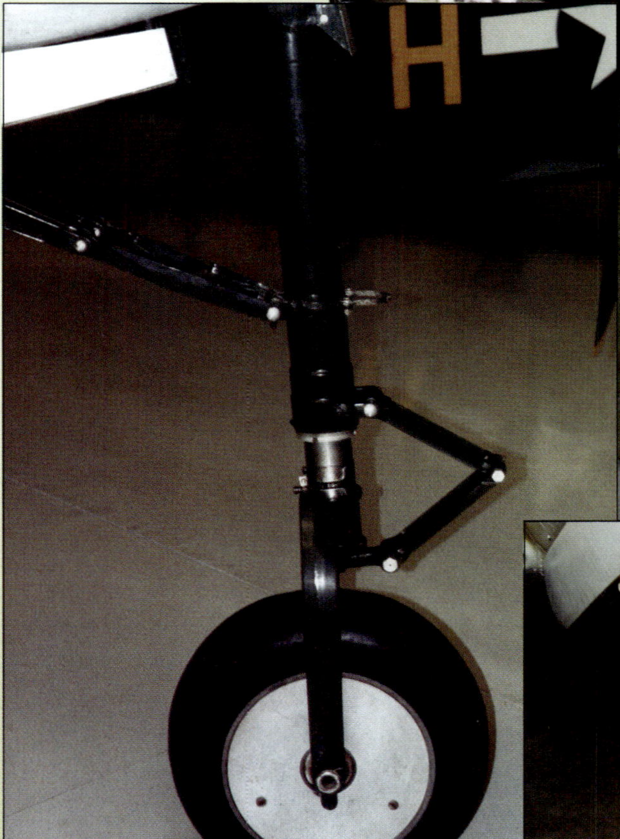

Bell P-39 In Detail

Above:
Nose gear wheel well.

Right:
Port side of the nose wheel.

Details of the nose undercarriage gear leg.

(All photos A. Loche)

Two photos of the nose undercarriage leg and wheel. (Wojciech Łuczak)

Above:
Nose undercarriage gear door.

Right:
Details of the nose wheel well, looking aft. (Photos A. Lochte)

Below:
Crewmen of the 71st Tactical Reconnaissance Group and their aircraft on an airfield in New Guinea, 1944. Note that fourth P-39 (from the right) has been fitted with the older balloon nose tire. Compare the size of the tire and wheel of the third aircraft in line, which has the low-profile nose tire. (Stratus coll.)

Armament

Above: P-39N, port side, .50-cal machine gun is visible. The pink box is a battery.
Below: Starboard side, 37-mm cannon ammunition rack is visible. The perforated panel is a feed door. The yellow tank is for oxygen. (Photos A. Lochte)

Bell P-39 In Detail

Two photos of the armament compartment of the P-39N. Note that .50 cal machine gun ammunition box is missing. Aircraft during restoration. (A. Lochte)

Above: Two photos of the Airacobra armament compartment. Photos from the Technical Manual.

P-39N. The 37 mm gun muzzle in the spinner. (A. Lochte)

37-mm gun ammunition box. (Wojciech Łuczak)

.30 cal. ammunition boxes
.30 cal. machine guns
.50 cal. machine guns
Blast tubes
Gun switches on control column
.37 mm. magazine
.37 mm. cannon
Switch box
30 cal. machine guns
30 cal. ammunition boxes

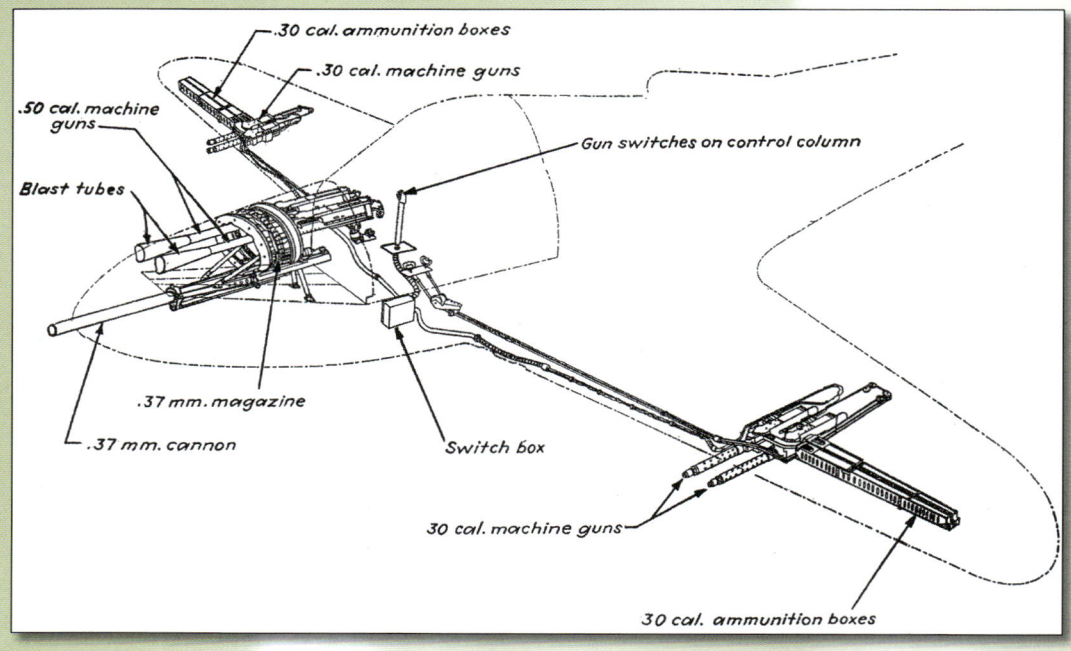

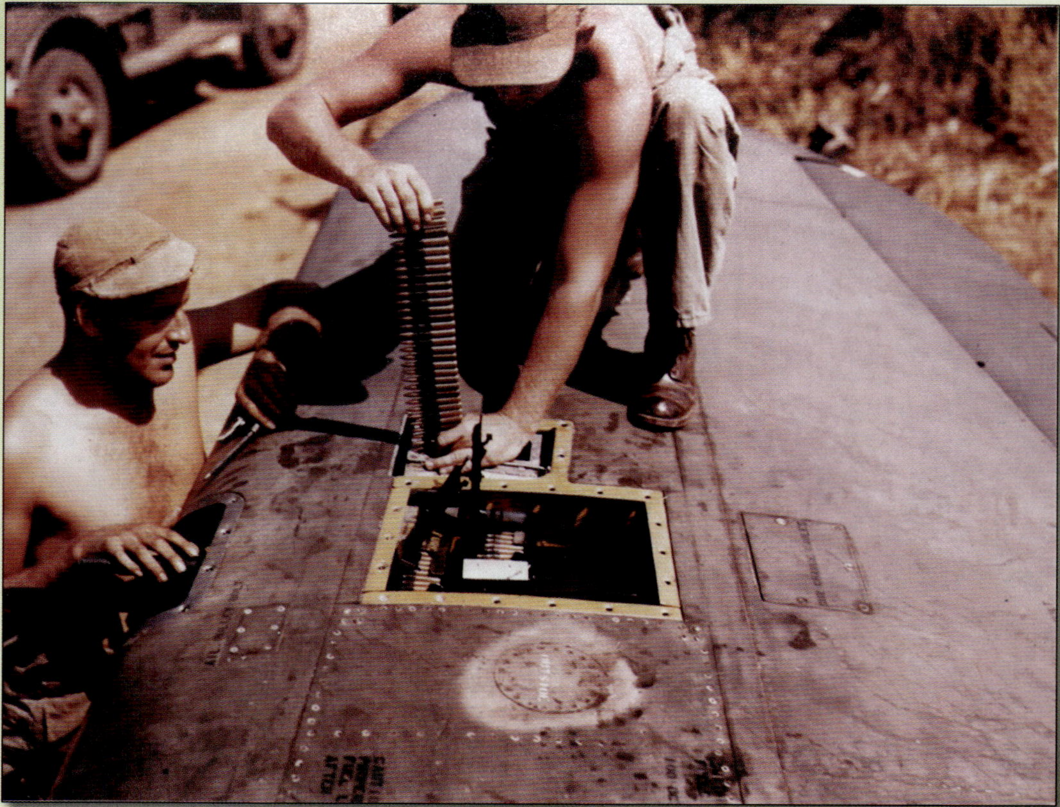

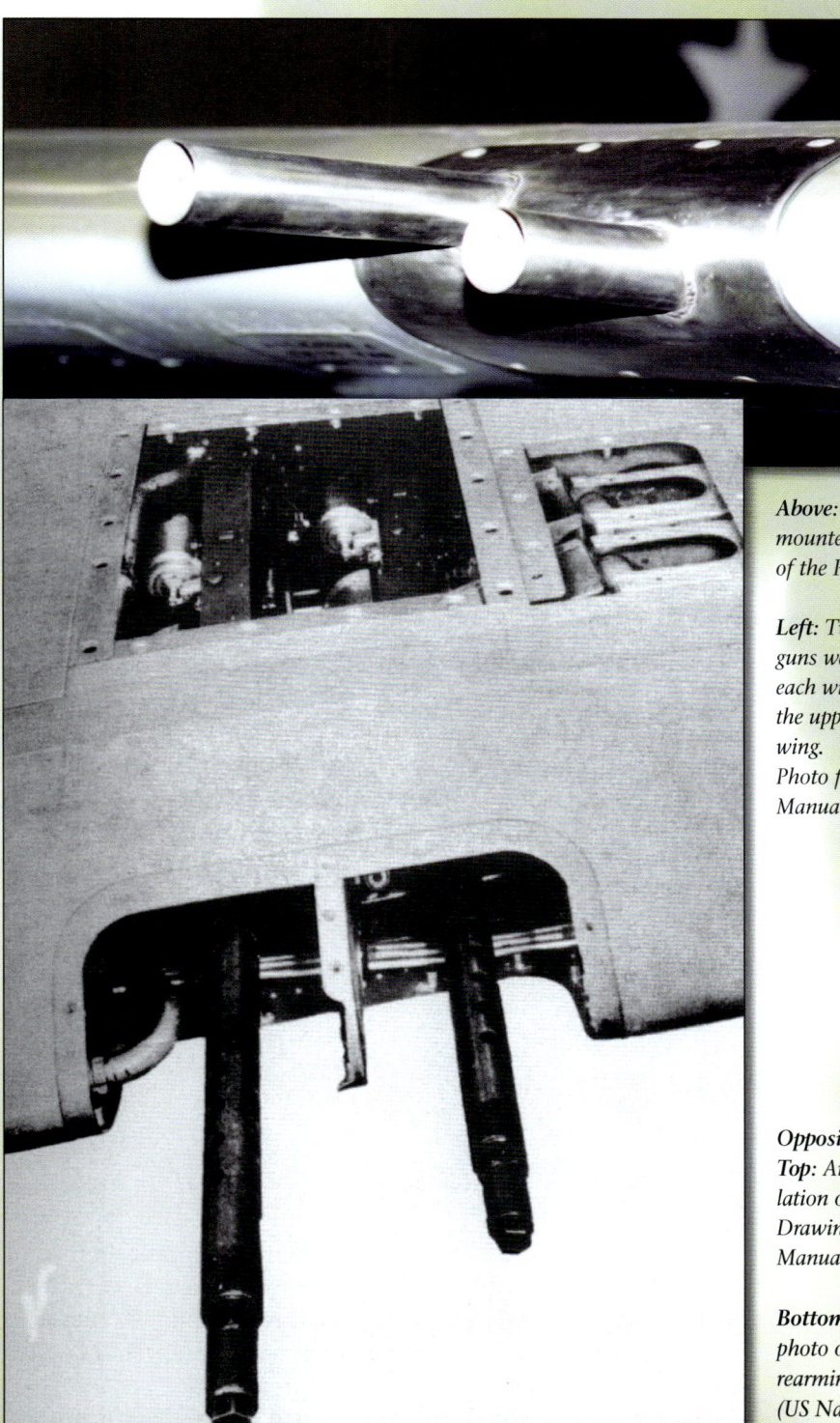

Above: Machine guns mounted in the port wing of the P-39N. (A. Lochte)

Left: Two .30 in machine guns were mounted in each wing. Front view of the upper side of the port wing.
Photo from the Technical Manual.

Opposite page:
Top: Armament installation of the P-39N. Drawing from Technical Manual.

Bottom: Period colour photo of the wing guns rearming.
(US National Archive)

Two photos of the bazooka rockets tests with a P-39N. (US National Archive)

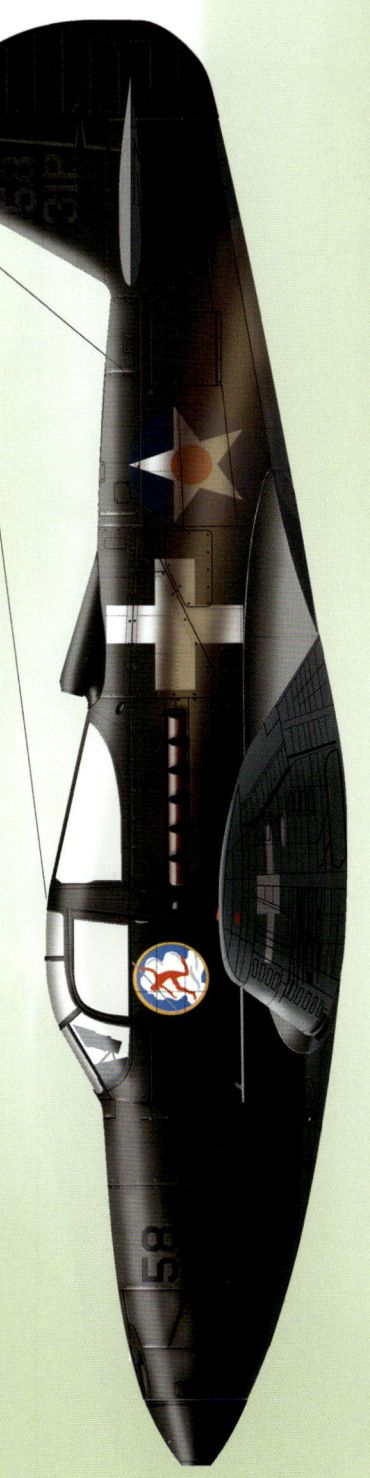

P-39C "58" of 40th PS, 31st PG during exercises at the end of 1941. White crosses were painted with removable paint. Olive Drab over Neutral Gray.

P-39C "22:31P" of 40th PS, Louisiana War Game Exercises "White Cross", April 1941. Olive Drab over Neutral Gray.

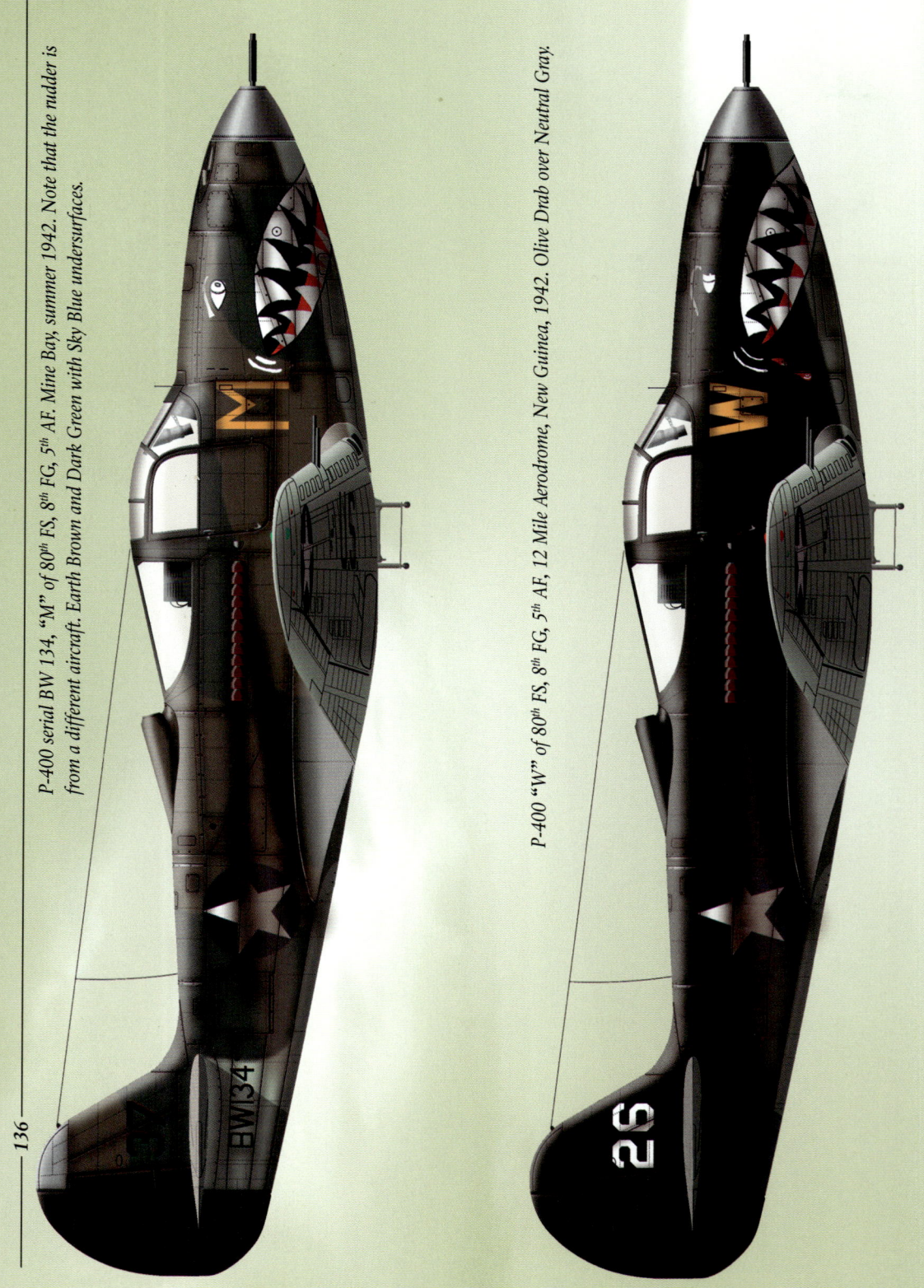

P-400 serial BW 134, "M" of 80th FS, 8th FG, 5th AF. Mine Bay, summer 1942. Note that the rudder is from a different aircraft. Earth Brown and Dark Green with Sky Blue undersurfaces.

P-400 "W" of 80th FS, 8th FG, 5th AF, 12 Mile Aerodrome, New Guinea, 1942. Olive Drab over Neutral Gray.

P-400 "K" of 80th FS, 8th FG, 5th AF, 12 Mile Aerodrome, New Guinea, 1942. Rudder in RAF camouflage is from a different aircraft. Olive Drab over Neutral Gray.

P-400 "F" of 80th FS, 8th FG, 5th AF, Milne Bay, end of 1942. Olive Drab over Neutral Gray.

P-400, serial BW 155, "24" of 67th FS, 347th FG, 13th AF, Henderson Field, Guadalcanal, October 1942. Personal aircraft of Lt. Barclay Dillon. Aircraft in RAF camouflage.

P-400, serial BW 156, "Fancy Nancy" of 67th FS, Guadalcanal, 1942. Aircraft in RAF camouflage.

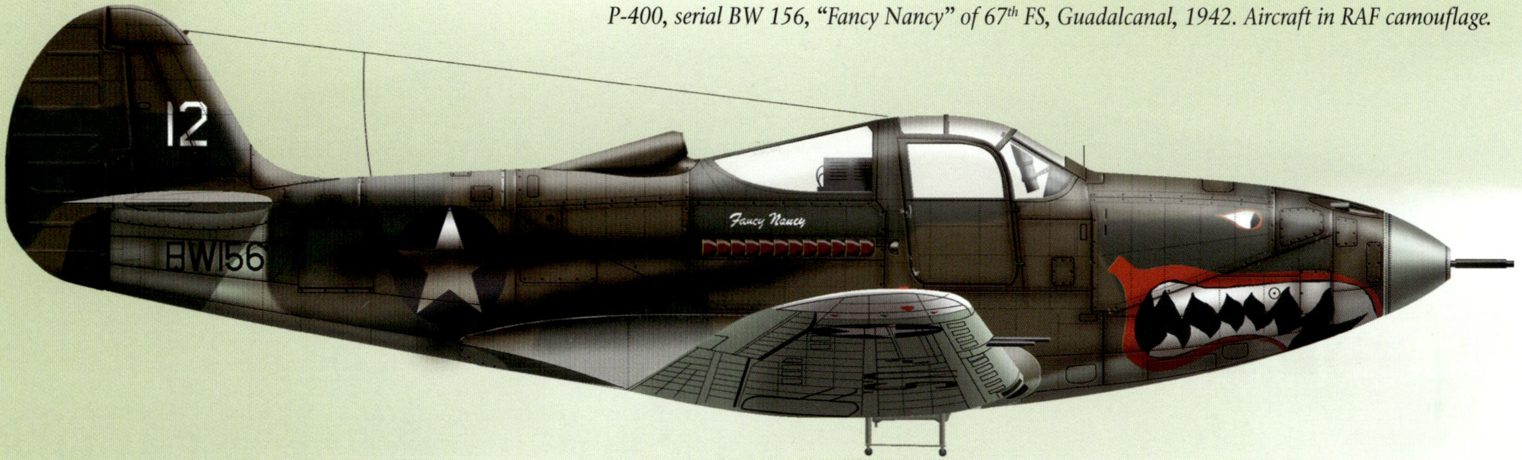

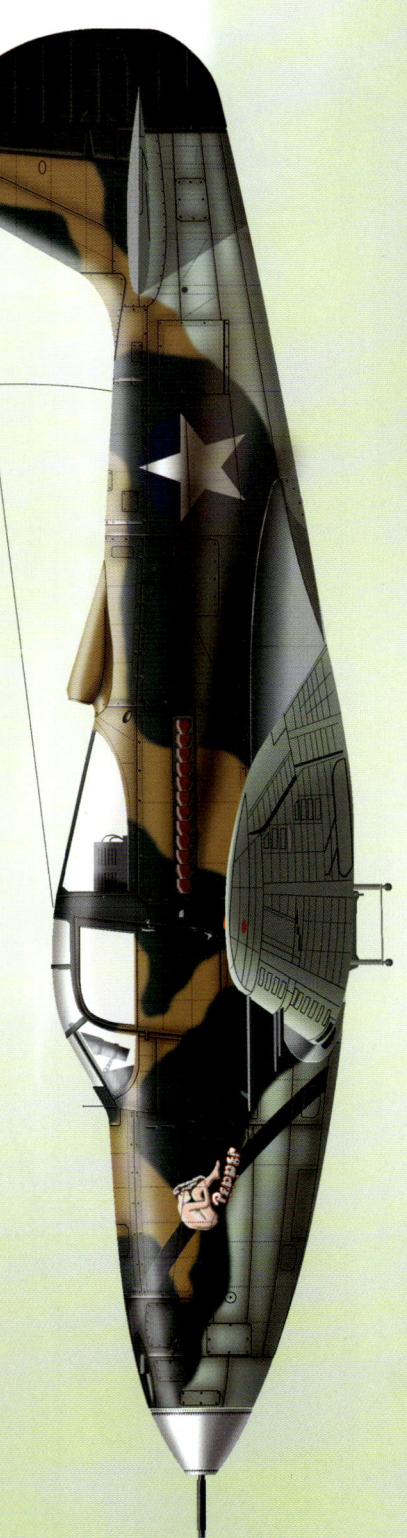

P-400 "80", "Pepper" of 67th FS, 347th FG, 13th AF, Guadalcanal, end of 1942. Aircraft in rather unusual camouflage.

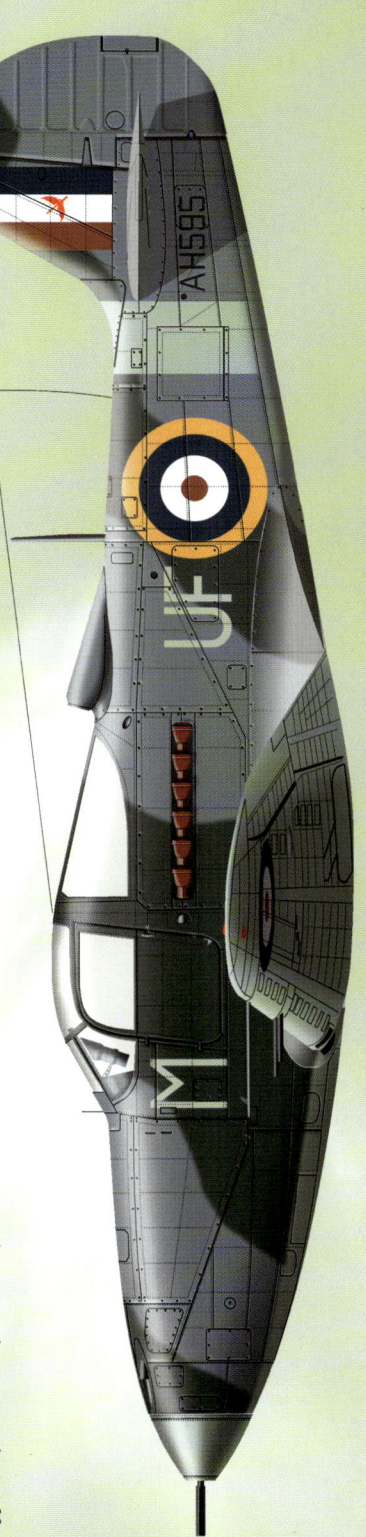

Airacobra Mk I serial AH595, UF-M of 601 Squadron RAF, Duxford 1941. Dark Green and Ocean Grey upper surface with Sky undersurface.

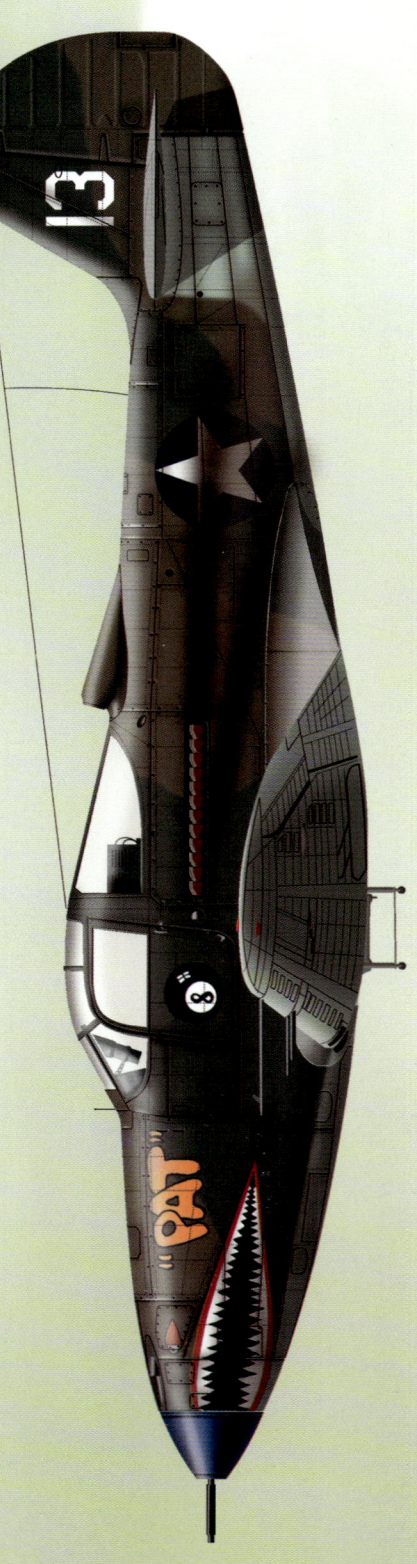

This and opposite page:
P-400 of 39th FS, 35th FG, 5th AF, 12 Mile Aerodrome New Guinea, 1942, personal aircraft of Lt. Eugene Wahl. Earth Brown with Dark Green upper surfaces with Sky undersurfaces.

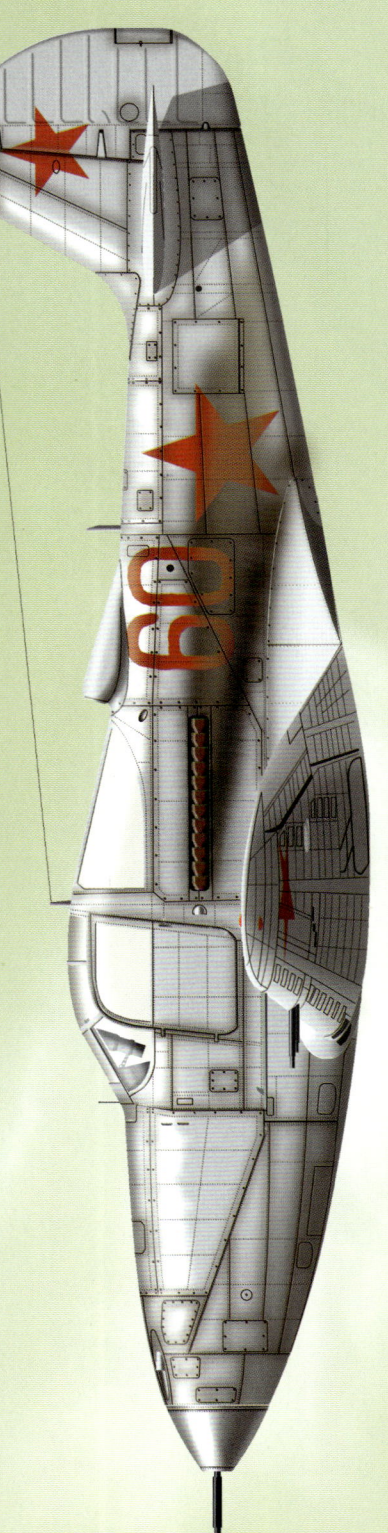

P-400 "60" of 2 GSAP winter 1942/43. Aircraft silver overall.

P-400 s/n 306, OK-G of Forsa Aerea Portuguesa, June 1943. RAF Camouflage.

Airacobra Mk I serial AH 636, of 19 GIAP. Aircraft in RAF camouflage. Personal aircraft of Capt. Ivan Gaydienko. He scored 7 individual victories plus 23 shared. Red stars are for personal victories, with white borders for shared ones.

P-39D-1 serial 41-38350, "P" of 35th FS, 8th FG, 5th AF, Milne Bay, New Guinea, October 1942. Personal aircraft of pilot Lt. I. A. Erickson. Olive Drab with Neutral Gray.

P-39D-1 serial 41-28297, "51" of 363rd Training Squadron, California 1942. Olive Drab with Neutral Gray.

P-39D-2 serial 41-7031, "816" of 51st FG, North Africa, summer 1943. Olive Drab with Neutral Gray.

P-39D-2 serial 41-38428, "37" of 16 GIAP, April 1943. Personal aircraft of Capt. Vadim Fadieyev, (18+3 victories). Olive Drab with Neutral Gray.

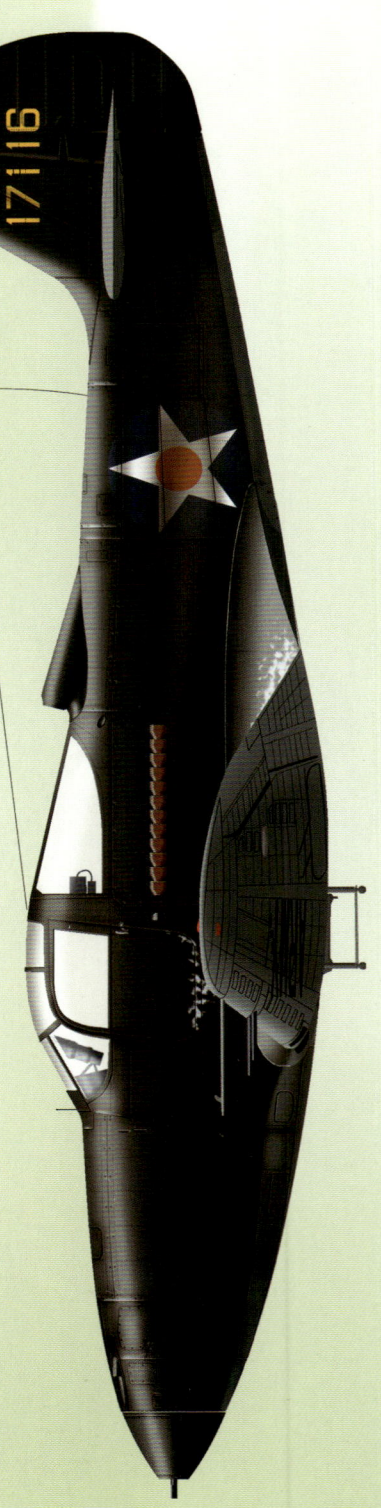

P-39F serial 41-7116 of 31st FS, 8th FG, Port Moresby, New Guinea, May 1942. Personal aircraft of Lt. G. Gowson. Olive Drab with Neutral Gray.

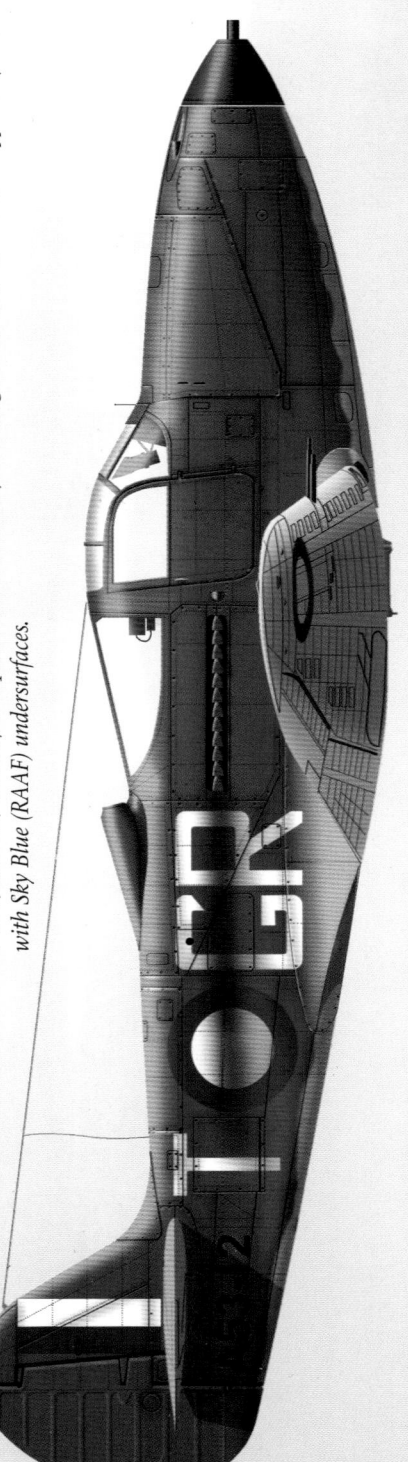

P-39F, A53-12, T-GR of 82 Squadron RAAF. Aircraft in Foliage Green and Earth Brown upper surfaces with Sky Blue (RAAF) undersurfaces.

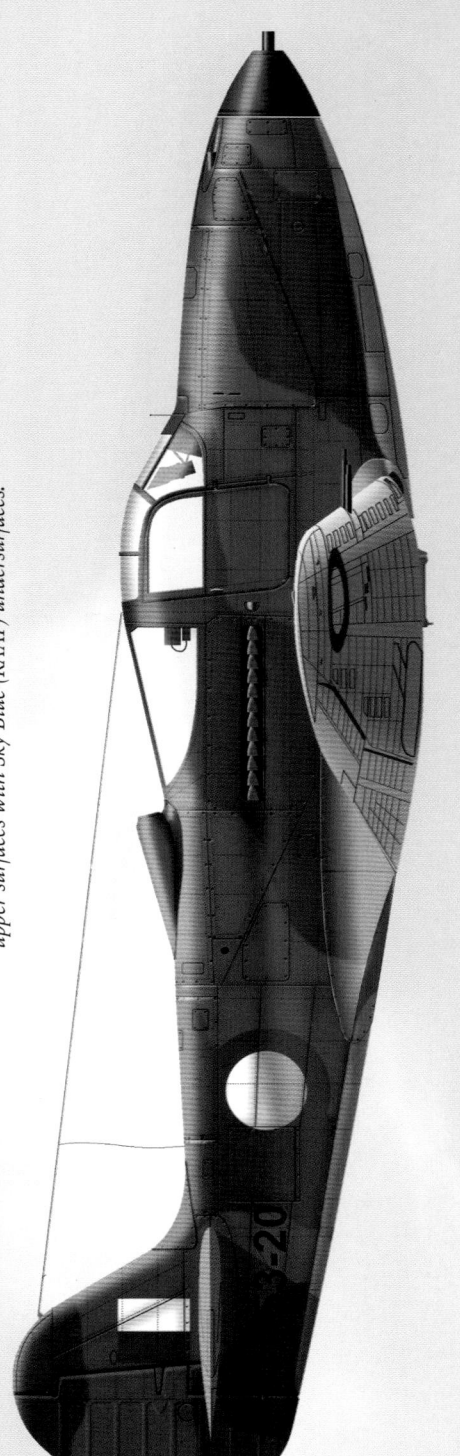

P-39F, A53-20 at 3 Aircraft Depot, July-September 1943. Aircraft in Foliage Green and Olive Drab upper surfaces with Sky Blue (RAAF) undersurfaces.

P-39F, A53-9, T-Z of 24 Squadron RAAF in late 1942. Aircraft Olive Drab upper surfaces with Sky Blue (RAAF) undersurfaces.

P-39J serial 41-7073 of 57th FS, 54th FG Alaska, August 1942. Personal aircraft of Lt. Lesli Spunts. Olive Drab with Neutral Gray.

P-39K-1 serial 42-4358 "23", "Grace" of 39th FS, 35th FG, 5th AF New Guinea, August 1942. Olive Drab with Neutral Gray.

P-39K-1 serial 42-4403 "21" of 45 IAP, Kuban, spring 1943. Personal aircraft of Lt. Dimitr Glinka (30 victories). Olive Drab with Neutral Gray.

P-39L-1 serial 42-4558 Q-T, "The Pantie Bandit" of 93rd FG, Tunisia 1943. Aircraft repainted in RAF desert camouflage.

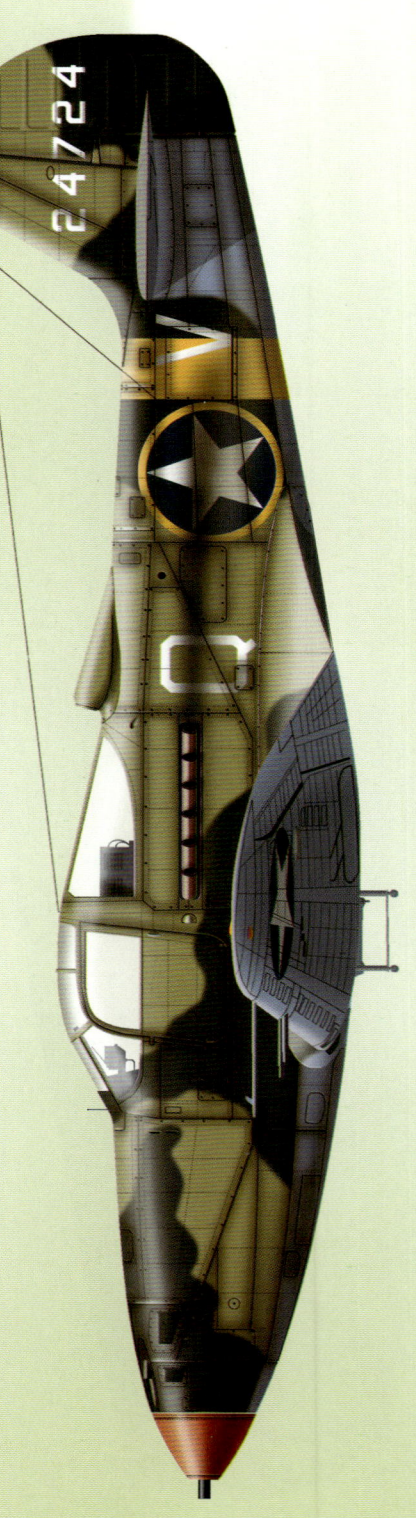

P-39M-1 serial 42-4724 Q-V, North Africa 1943. Aircraft repainted in RAF desert camouflage.

P-39N serial 42-9004 of 9 GIAD, 16 GIAP, Poland 1944. Personal aircraft of sub-Coll. Aleksandr Pokryshkin (59+3 victories). Olive Drab over Neutral Grey.

P-39N of 9 GIAP, August 1943. Personal aircraft of Kpt. Sultan Amet-khan. Olive Drab over Neutral Grey.

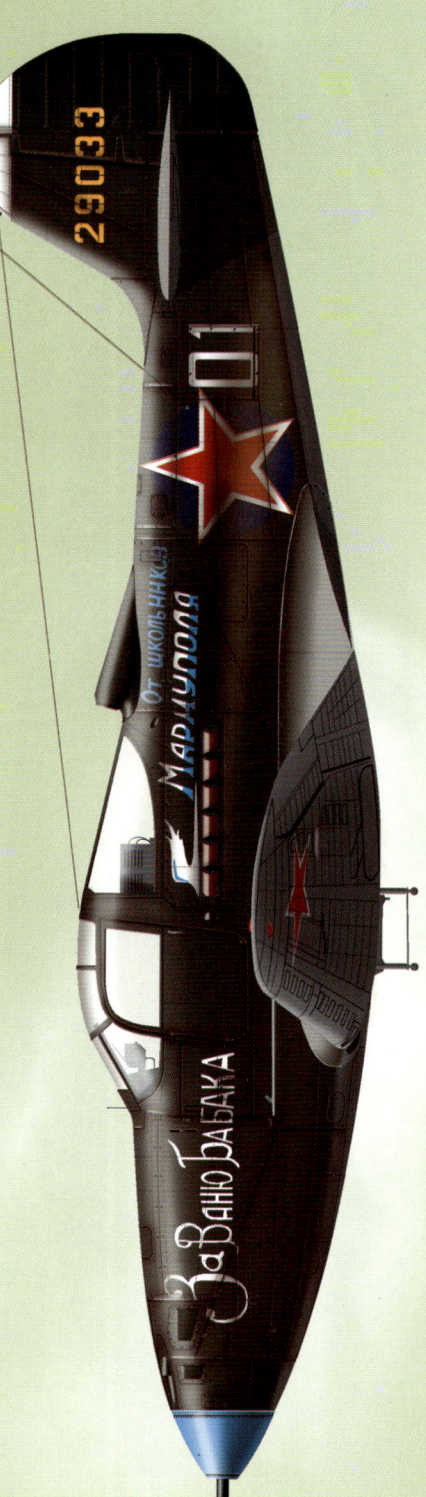

P-39N serial 42-9033, of 9 GIAD, 100 GIAP, Germany, May 1945. Personal aircraft of Gieorgiy Dolnikov (15+1 victories). Earlier it was the personal aircraft of Capt. Ivan Babak (33+4 victories), who become POW on 22 April 1945. Olive Drab over Neutral Grey.

P-39N of 191 IAP, Leningrad Front, summer 1944. Olive Drab over Neutral Grey.

P-39N of 16 GIAP, Germany, April 1945. Personal aircraft of Lt. Konstantin Suchov. Olive Drab over Neutral Grey.

P-39N-1 serial 42-9434 of 9 GIAD, 16 GIAP, Poland, October 1944. Personal aircraft of Capt. Aleksandr Klubov (11+16 victories). Olive Drab over Neutral Grey.

P-39N-1 serial 42-9377 "19" of the Italian Co-Belligerent Air Force, 1943/44. Olive Drab over Neutral Grey.

P-39N-5-BE serial 42-18769 of GC I/4 "Navarre", 1 Escadrille at Meknes Algeria, June 1943. Olive Drab over Neutral Grey.

P-39N-5-BE serial 42-18736 of GC I/4 "Navarre" at La Reghaia Algeria, November 1943. Major Commandant Joseph Machot de La Martiniere. Olive Drab over Neutral Grey.

P-39N-5 serial 42-18738) "A" of GC I/4 "Navarre", 1944. Olive Drab over Neutral Grey.

P-39Q-1 serial 41-19447 "O" Personal aircraft of the 357th FG commander, Edward S. Chickering during training at Marysville (California) in July 1943. Olive Drab over Neutral Grey.

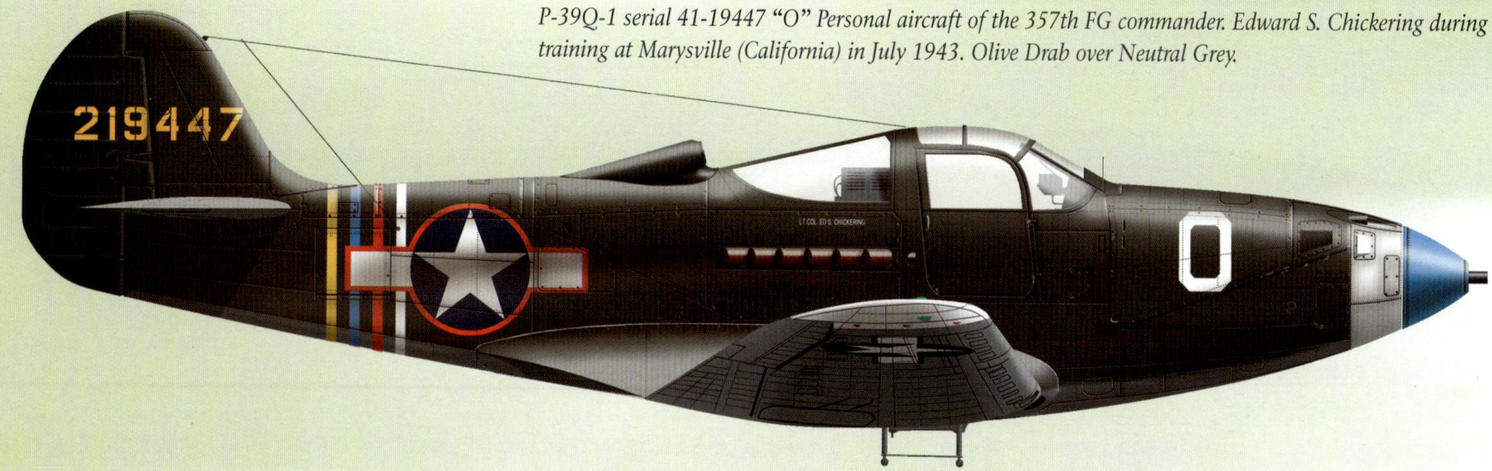

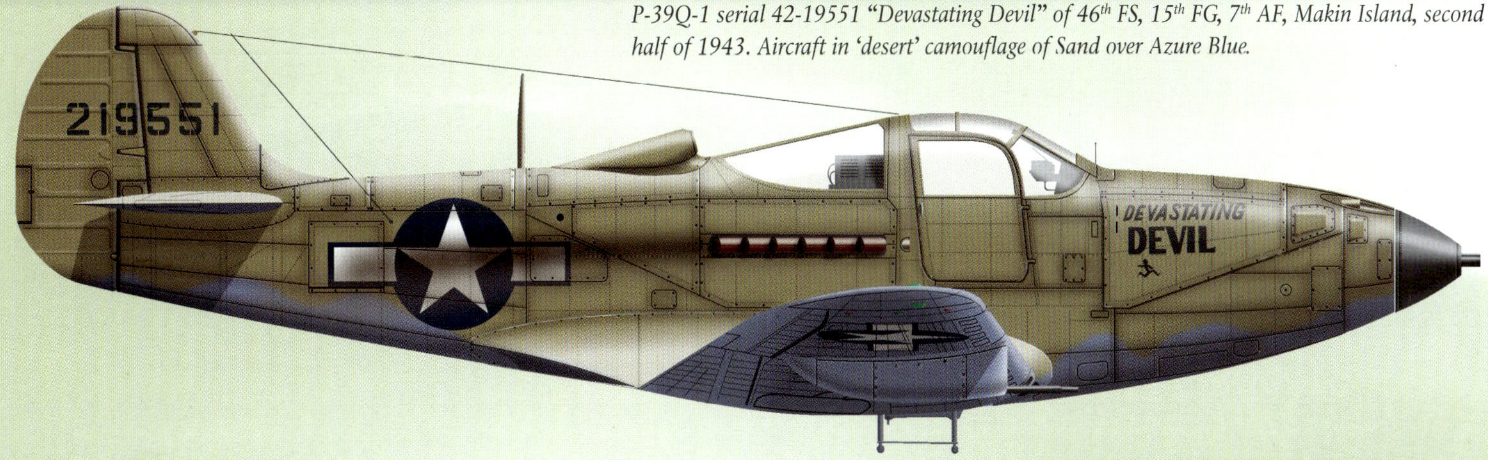

P-39Q-1 serial 42-19551 "Devastating Devil" of 46th FS, 15th FG, 7th AF, Makin Island, second half of 1943. Aircraft in 'desert' camouflage of Sand over Azure Blue.

P-39Q-10 serial 42-20746 of 363rd FS, 357th FG, California 1943. Personal aircraft of Lt. Bud Anderson. Olive Drab over Neutral Grey.

P-39Q-15 "67" of 72 GIAP, summer 1944. Olive Drab over Neutral Grey.

P-39Q-25-BE serial 44-32451 of GC I/5 "Champagne", 1 Esc. at Salon-de-Provance, October 1944. Olive Drab over Neutral Grey.

P-39Q-25 44-32286 of 213 GIAP, Poland, September 1944. Personal aircraft of Lt. Nikalay Stroikov (14+21 victories). Olive Drab over Neutral Grey.

P-39Q of 100 GIAP, summer 1944. Personal aircraft of Lt. Petr Gutshek (18+3 victories). Olive Drab over Neutral Grey.

P-39Q of 19 GIAP, end of 1943. Personal aircraft of Capt. Pavel Kutashov (13+28 victories). Olive Drab over Neutral Grey.

P-39Q, the only Polish Airacobra, personal aircraft of Gen. Fiodor Połynin (Russian nationality) – Commander of the Polish Air Force in 1944 – 1947.